Street and

working children

A GUIDE TO PLANNING

By Judith Ennew

DEVELOPMENT MANUAL 4

Save the Children

Save the Children Development Manual No. 4

Published by
Save the Children
Mary Datchelor House
17 Grove Lane
London SE5 8RD

ISBN: 1 870322 82 7
ISSN: 0966-6982 Save the Children Development Manuals

Design and page make-up by Devious Designs
Typeset by Nancy White
Printed by Page Bros

CONTENTS

Chapter 1

INTRODUCTION

Projects for street and working children often seem to be reinventing the wheel, which not infrequently turns out to be square rather than round. Although there are thousands of such projects worldwide, and workshops and conferences to discuss the problem have proliferated at a tremendous rate in the past decade, simple practical issues seem more often than not to be obscured in rhetoric. Despite so much accumulated experience there is very little commonsense advice easily available in readable form. It is difficult to get hold of literature and harder still to evaluate it. This manual aims to provide a starting point for anyone wishing to begin or improve projects with street and working children.

Over the past decade or so, street children have become almost fashionable. They are highly visible on the modern streets of cities in the South. Increased global travel has made tourists and business travellers aware of them. They are widely photographed and described – they make good copy for newspapers, with powerful images evoking pity at their plight and envy of their freedom. There have been a number of films and documentaries, most notably Mira Nair's *Salaam Bombay* and Hector Babenco's *Pixote*. Many international development agencies have based successful fundraising campaigns on images of street children.

Compared with this, working children have an image problem. In the industrialised countries people tend to think of the nineteenth century, of chimney sweeps and children down mines, and of successful campaigns to abolish child labour. Yet millions of children work now in agriculture, workshops, factories and as domestic servants. They are not as visible as street children. It can be difficult to gain access to them and take photographs, and even when they are photographed the pictures seldom have the same emotional impact.

Thus there are few projects aimed directly at working children and many thousands that work with street children. Yet all street children are in some sense working, in that they manage to get the means of daily survival together. Many simply work on the streets, as shoeshiners or vendors for instance, attending school and going home at night to their families. These are not the wild abandoned street children of the popular image. However, it is difficult to separate the two types, which causes problems for project planning.

This manual looks at the planning process for both visible and invisible children. If it has a bias, it is towards the more visible urban children of developing countries. This is partly because there is more project experience in this area to draw on, and many of the lessons learned can be extended to work with other children. It is also difficult to ignore children working and living on the street and this can be the initial stimulus to begin projects with them, which may be developed later with their less conspicuous contemporaries.

STRUCTURE OF THIS MANUAL

Each chapter of this manual may be read as a separate unit, although if it is read from start to finish it should provide a guide to planning projects for street and working children. It begins by assuming that the reader knows very little about the topic, but has been moved by the plight of these children and wishes to know how to do something to improve their lives and to learn from the experiences of other projects. Because it is intended as a basic guide, material in some chapters may already be familiar to some readers. But if you are starting from scratch it is wiser to take nothing for granted.

The chapters cover what is known in general about street and working children; using secondary data to find out what is already known in the local situation; researching new information on the local situation; types of projects, and how to set them up; organising human resources in project development; and the most common problems encountered in working with street children.

At the end of Chapters 2 to 6, a set of questions is provided that sums up what has been covered, and Appendix 1 provides a checklist and flow chart to help with the planning process (see page 168), and a brief guide to further reading can be found in Appendix 3 (see page 175).

WORKING WITH, NOT FOR, CHILDREN

There are more questions than answers in this manual. It is not a 'how to' guide for day to day work in a project for street and working children. It does not set out a model project. Although it draws on the experiences of many projects worldwide it will not be using any of these as models, but more as examples of what can be and has been done in various settings and with different resources.

All those experiences have led to one fundamental conclusion: children are capable, resourceful people whose individual histories, feelings and opinions must be respected. It follows that projects must be considered always as working *with* children rather than *for* them, encouraging and facilitating the fullest possible participation.

THE CHILDREN'S VIEW

We would like to finish going to school in order to fulfil our ambitions and have a bright future. We also wish to have our own houses so we will have a place for shelter and sleep We would also like to help other street children so they won't be wandering in the streets anymore and so they won't sniff solvent. We also wish to be healthy so we can help our country. We also wish to have a new life so that our future children will be properly guided and most of all, we wish to have a prosperous and peaceful life because if life is peaceful, there won't be any street children.

(Open letter from Street Children to Fellow Children, *Proceedings of the First Metro Manila Street Children's Conference*, 1990, p71)

A NOTE ON REFERENCES

For readers interested in following up some of the writers quoted or mentioned in this manual, a list of the books and articles that are referred to is given at the end, with the authors and organisations mentioned in alphabetical and date order. For example, an article by Benno Glauser published 1990, will appear in the text as (Glauser, 1990, p400) and in the list of references as 'Glauser, B, Street children: deconstructing a construct', with the further information that this is an article in a book edited by Allison James and Alan Prout, and the publication details – 'in James, A & Prout, A (eds) *Constructing and deconstructing childhood: contemporary issues in the sociological study of childhood*, London, New York, Philadelphia, The Falmer Press, 1990'. Organisations and other bodies that are quoted will appear in the same list. Thus 'Proceedings of the First Metro Manila Street Children's Conference' will be listed under 'Proceedings...'. Unpublished sources are not included in the reference list as they are usually extremely difficult to obtain. In some cases where no reference is provided, the information has been given verbally by the named individual involved.

Although there are many publications about street and working children they are not all useful for programme planning, and unfortunately some of the better work is either unpublished or difficult to get hold of. This is the case with some of the references used for this manual, which is why the list of references is followed by a guide to further reading on specific topics that provides a set of easy to obtain texts, and details of how to obtain them.

A NOTE ON SOURCES

One of the greatest disgraces of the modern world is that, although people know about *the existence* of street and working children, relatively little is known about *the conditions of their lives*, much less their own worries and aspirations. There are many projects to help them worldwide, but there is surprisingly little sharing of information and experiences. Countless books and reports have been written, but much of this is descriptive and often voyeuristic. Many projects have been written about, but this is often through the project's own perspective or from its promotional literature, making every project sound like a success. Meanwhile there seems to be little overall improvement in the general situation of street and working children, despite increasing interest over the past decade. Indeed, my own gut feeling, after nearly 15 years in the field, is that things are getting worse for children everywhere.

My purpose in writing this manual is to try to disseminate experiences of colleagues with whom I have been working during that time to a wider group of people. Some examples are from Save the Children projects, others from a variety of different agencies and backgrounds. I have visited or had contact with almost all the projects mentioned; in some cases the contact has been maintained over several years. With very few exceptions, I know personally the people whose experiences are discussed in this manual. Many are close friends. All are committed not only to the improvement of children's lives but also to the importance of listening to children and taking their perspective. I could not have thought of writing this manual without their openness in sharing their ideas, hopes, frustrations and sometimes failures with me over many years. Their names appear in the following pages. I hope they will accept my thanks and that I am able to give the best possible account of their work. I am particularly indebted to ongoing discussions with Jo Boyden, Benno Glauser, Don Kaminsky, Nandana Reddy and Jill Swart. Special thanks are due to Mark Connolly, who has not only shared his experiences but also read and commented on drafts of the manual. Of course the responsibility for both opinions and mistakes is all mine.

It has almost become a tradition for the author of a publication on street children to thank the children and dedicate it to them, referring to memories of their companionship, friendship and the fun they had together. But street and working children cannot read this manual – and there is no place in it for sentimental tokenism. They already have too many burdens to bear.

Chapter 2

UNDERSTANDING STREET AND WORKING CHILDREN

There are two basic rules for work with any children:
- The main barrier to successful programmes is our own attitudes.
- The main resource in any project is the children themselves.

When projects aim to help street and working children these rules become particularly important. Adults tend to think about children in terms of providing for and protecting them. The dominant notion of childhood in child welfare programmes insists that children should live in loving families, playing and going to school, free from adult cares and responsibilities. So children who work rather than go to school and spend their time on the streets instead of with their families bring out a rush of protective feelings – the first instinct is to rescue them.

Children have little say in what happens in society, and adults tend to assume that they know what is in the children's 'best interests'. But children who have been taking a good deal of responsibility for themselves, and probably also for others, often have definite ideas about what is best for them. The problem is that few people listen to them or use their skills and capacities.

CONFRONTING YOUR OWN ATTITUDES

It is not always easy to untangle the ideas we have about children. It means thinking back to our own early experiences, considering our own children, and also thinking about cultural notions of childhood that we take for granted. But it is worth asking a few basic questions.

What is a child?

The majority of the information about 'children' actually deals with the health of children under five years of age (pre-school). Most national and international statistics can give only school enrolment or attendance data for children between five and 15 years. Then there is a flurry of interest in 'youth' over 15 as they are legally able to get wage labour jobs, and are also thought of as a problem group

– involved in 'sex and drugs and rock and roll'. As programmes dealing with street children usually try to target the 5 to 15-year-olds, the lack of information about this age group is a problem in itself.

Some programmes divide children into age groups such as infants (0-5 years), school-age (6-15 years) and youth (15-18 years). But there are many pitfalls and problems in these categories if they are used arbitrarily or without taking account of local ideas about children and childhood.

The Convention on the Rights of the Child (adopted by the United Nations in 1989) defines a child as anyone under the age of 18 years. The reason for this is that, in most countries, this is the age at which citizenship really begins, when you can vote for the legislation and policies that rule your life. Universally, therefore, a child is not a citizen and has no political power.

In other spheres children are also defined by age and by what they are *not*. They are not workers, they are not sexual, not married, not parents, they are not smokers, drinkers, car drivers or able to sign contracts. What they *are* is quite limited – they are in families, they go to school, they play. They are preparing to become adults.

Culturally, developed societies are contradictory about children. For centuries Western thinkers have argued about whether or not they are born as little innocent angels who must be protected from the wicked world of adults, or born in original sin so that adults have to control them and make sure the evil is exorcised. Besides the arguments about this it also seems possible to hold both ideas simultaneously. Whatever the case, there seems to be something special about the way childhood is thought of, as if it is closer to nature, with more happiness and more freedom.

Are all childhoods the same?

Happy, carefree childhood is the story as far as childhood in industrialised countries and richer families everywhere is concerned (and it was largely countries of the North that drafted the Convention). In poor communities in the South many people younger than 18 years (quite a lot younger in many cases):

- work for their living and may be supporting parents, grandparents, siblings, a partner or even their own children;
- smoke (sometimes more than tobacco), drink alcohol and have sexual relations;
- care for younger children, of employers, of parents and often of their own;
- fight willingly for political causes, take part in political demonstrations and debates, and may be imprisoned and tortured because they do so;
- are not living with their own families, but with an employer, a partner, alone

or with a group on the street;
- do not go to school because: they are working, there is no school, they cannot afford it, the curriculum is irrelevant, they cannot understand the language the teachers are using, they have already been marked as school failures, their parents will not send them, it is 'not worth' educating a girl.

Child labour

One problem is that international legislation, and international aid agencies, tend to work with a global model of childhood based on middle-class children in the North (and the South), who *do* go to school, play, live in increasingly private families and are assumed to be helpless and not able to carry out adult tasks. This means that programmes for poor children in the South assume that this is normal and that all children are weak and powerless. Children who work hard, long hours and take a good deal of responsibility are not seen as capable human beings, but pitied because they are not having a 'childhood'. Thus, policies may aim at abolishing work. But this may not be the best option. Children often need to work and are proud of their independence and the contribution they make to their own, and their families', upkeep

It is useful to think about who defines child labour as a problem. For governments and international agencies it may be a problem because it is against the law or contrary to international standards. For parents and children it may be a problem if there is not enough work, or the pay is not good enough. Some children may enjoy work and not see it as a problem at all, until perhaps in later life they want to progress and find themselves held back by lack of education. For others work is so hard, so dull, so dreary that the whole of their childhood is a problem because of it.

Children's capacities

Reliance on a model of childhood based on children in better-off families ignores the very real strengths and actual experiences of working and street children. It leads to an attitude of pity, rather than empathy, which is reflected in projects that try to rescue children from work and the street without thinking of the consequences for the children or their families. Families may need the income provided by the child. Children can be proud of the work that they do and the contribution they make, or the fact that they support themselves. They may need help, but this needs to be on their own terms and in the context of the lives they lead, otherwise even more harm may be done.

Jo Boyden points out that what children are 'capable of' depends on the culture in which they live:

> ... while in many countries children are seen as dependent until well into their teens, in many others they are expected to be fully independent from an early age. The contrast between Britain and Peru, for example, is instructive. In the former it is illegal to leave infants and small children in charge of juveniles under the age of 14. In the latter, on the other hand, the national census records a significant group of 6 to 14-year-olds who are heads of households and as such are the principal breadwinners in the family, sometimes even the sole person in charge of the care of younger siblings (Boyden, 1990, p198).

People in the North, whose children are well protected, find it easy enough to think of children in their teens working and being separated from their families, but hard to believe that even small children can successfully shoulder quite heavy burdens of responsibility. Children may start working with and for their families well before they might be expected to begin school. They help in family market stalls and shops and do many domestic tasks. Thomas Weisner's work among the Abaluya in Kenya shows that the great majority of childcare is children's work rather than women's work (Weisner, 1989). When mothers have to go out to work in urban settings then children become housewives in their stead. It is far from unusual to find a 5-year-old at home alone caring for two younger children, and making a pretty good job of it too.

In the match and firework industry of Sivakasi, India, children start work as young as four or five years old. They are bussed in from rural areas, which gives them a 12-14 hour day. Their parents, who need the cash income, also feel the children are learning useful skills. In street work the usual age to begin being an independent earner, as a shoeshiner for instance, is around eight years of age, although it may be earlier. Many children pay for their own school books and uniforms in this way.

Although the one universal defining characteristic of children is that they have no legitimate political power, there are obviously different stages in childhood. It must make a difference whether a child starts its career on the street at 6, 10 or 14 years of age. If you start work at three years of age you are unlikely ever to start school; if you start at 14 you may already be literate, numerate and have a number of skills. There are different dangers involved in working with heavy weights or toxic substances as a toddler, before and at puberty, and in your teens. Overall lifetime chances are fundamentally governed by such questions.

HELPING STREET AND WORKING CHILDREN

Because people feel that they must rescue children from working or from the streets, there is a tendency to think in terms of providing for them and protecting them. Thus a common reaction is to start by handing out food and clothes, or by building an orphanage. The problem with these reactions, as we shall see later, is that they fail to provide lasting solutions. Instead they create dependency. In order to plan for developmental solutions, in which people confront their problems, tackle the root causes and find their own solutions, it is necessary to examine some of the most common mistaken ideas about street and working children.

The street child image

STREET CHILDREN: THE PUBLIC IMAGE

They spend the nights anywhere in the streets, stay up late, get little sleep, are exposed to passers-by as abandoned, homeless, tramps, thieves or juvenile delinquents (Glauser, 1990, pp140-141).

The children usually called street children seem to have the very opposite of a childhood. Many adults ignore them or think of them as a social nuisance. Others want to rescue them. They are certainly mythical figures, either because they seem to be romantically free from adult worries, or because they appear to be particularly immoral or unusually pathetic victims. But they are not just outlaw or waif figures photographed as part of the urban scenery. They are individual children, each with his or her own history, problems, necessities and hopes. Popular images of street children are one extra problem that they simply don't need. Some object to being called 'street children' because of the negative connotations; others act up to the image, especially for tourists and photographers.

Some popular perceptions about street children concerning their families, futures and the children themselves are noted here:

About their families
- they have been abandoned by their families;
- they have run away from home because of sexual abuse;
- they are the result of the breakdown of the family;

- their families have disintegrated because of poverty;
- their fathers are abusive alcoholics;
- they come from mother-headed families;
- they have no contact with their families.

About their futures
- they will grow up to be criminals;
- they will not survive to adulthood;
- they cannot be rehabilitated;
- they turn into terrorists and revolutionaries.

About the children
- they are starving;
- they are thieves;
- they have no choice but to be prostitutes;
- they are uncontrollably violent;
- they have lost all ability to feel emotions such as love;
- they do not know how to play;
- they have no morals;
- they are drug addicts;
- they have Aids.

Some of these ideas do apply to *some* children on the street *some* of the time. Others are untrue or unproven, but all of them have been applied to youngsters on the street at one time or another. Some ideas are more characteristic of Northern observers. Others, such as the assumption that they are criminals and terrorists in the making, have been used by local groups as justification for campaigns of violence against children on the street.

Such strongly negative views result from the difficulties experienced by modern, middle-class adults trying to come to terms with the fact that what they are confronted with is children who simply don't fit the modern image of childhood. It is threatening to adults to have to think about children who, just maybe, manage without them. Thus, in the early 1980s, the Inter-NGO Programme for Street Children and Street Youth described street children as being in 'a situation in which there is no protection, supervision or direction from responsible adults' as if this, in itself, were the problem. Perhaps this is why other commentators, including aid workers, academics and journalists, frequently refer to fictional tales of children living without parents. Sometimes they evoke romantically free children such as Mark Twain's Huckleberry Finn and Dickens' Artful Dodger, sometimes the dark picture drawn by William Golding in *Lord of the Flies*.

Current attempts to define street children

Anyone who is thinking of working with street children comes up sooner rather than later against the problem of definition. Two dominant versions attempt to distinguish between 'real' street children and children who are working on the street but return home to their families at night. The first is the definition drawn up by the Inter-NGO Programme for Street Children and Street Youth in the early 1980s:

> Street children are those for whom the street (in the widest sense of the word: ie unoccupied dwellings, wasteland etc) more than their family has become their real home, a situation in which there is no protection, supervision or direction from responsible adults.

Somewhat later in the 1980s, Unicef suggested a distinction between children *on* the streets and children *of* the streets, derived largely from experience in Latin America.

> Children *on* the streets are those 'whose family support base has become increasingly weakened [who] must share in the responsibility for family survival by working on city streets and marketplaces. For these children … the home ceases to be their centre for play, culture and daily life. Nevertheless while the street becomes their daytime activity, most of these children will return home most nights. While their family relationships may be deteriorating, they are still definitely in place, and these children continue to view life from the point of view of their families.'
>
> Children *of* the streets are 'a much smaller number of children who daily struggle for survival without family support, alone. While often called "abandoned", they too might also have abandoned their families, tired of insecurity and rejection and aged up with violence … [their] ties with home have now been broken … *de facto* [they] are without families' (Taçon, 1985, pp3 and 4).

As a further refinement, some documents of Unicef and other agencies separate 'abandoned' children who have no ties whatsoever with their families from other children 'of' the street, who have 'chosen the street as their home' and only have 'occasional' contacts with their families.

Trying to use these definitions

These original formulations of the distinction have been reworked many times, and there has probably been more written about this aspect of street children than any other. The 'in' and 'on' the streets formula, in its several guises, has worked for some projects, and at times proved useful from an operational point of view, particularly within Latin America. In Honduras, for example, Project Alternatives uses it as the basis of service delivery to two groups of children. The first are those who work with their parents in the vast markets of Tegucigalpa. The second group, with a distinct profile of problems, is made up of children living almost entirely separate from their families and not so associated with the markets.

IN HONDURAS, PROJECT ALTERNATIVES INTERPRETS THE UNICEF DISTINCTION

Children 'in' the street 'are boys and girls who work (usually for their mothers) as vendors in the markets or at some other market-based economic activity (carrying bags, begging, hauling away garbage, and the like); these children retain some contact with their families and live, however loosely, with some degree of parental (or adult) supervision'.

Children 'of' the street ... 'in contrast, are mostly teenagers who have been orphaned or abandoned by or run away from families, and who consider the streets to be their home. True abandoned street children are too young to enter the legitimate labor force and too estranged from their families to participate in the family's economic activities; they pass their time by sniffing glue, "hanging out", and participating in various forms of petty criminal activity. Thus, children in the streets are primarily market children, and children of the streets are primarily abandoned children. The latter are truly homeless and (more to the point, perhaps) without families; the former are not' (Wright, Kaminsky & Wittig, 1993, p280).

Nevertheless, project workers in some other parts of the world do not find the Unicef distinction so easy to apply. In India, for example, they ask where children living on pavements with their families fit into the picture.

> The whole categorisation is confused by entire families living permanently on the street. The terminology used by Unicef ... 'children of the street' ... 'children on the street' ... is confusing. Their third category, 'abandoned children', cannot be a category by itself but a sub-category ... along with 'estranged and runaway children' (Reddy, 1992, p3).

Another problem is that, when the same terms are used internationally, they are not necessarily applied in the same way to local circumstances, and this leads to many different interpretations of life 'in' and 'of' the street.

The meanings of 'street children' and 'children "on" and "of" the street' are not always clear and there is a danger that people will talk past each other, even within the same project. This is a problem for both research and project planning and for children who do not fit the label, who may miss out on service provision altogether.

Even in Latin America, where the distinction was first drawn, it is not always simple. Benno Glauser, who with his wife and a group of friends started a project in Asunción called Callescuela (Street School), says that he had many problems. Although the formula worked at an instinctive level on a day-to-day basis, he just could not distinguish two clear categories of street child. He asks how to categorise children who live in the streets on weekdays only, but go home at weekends, or those who only live out in warm summer weather. Some children whom he thought of as 'in' the streets actually stayed away from home for long periods of time. Others 'of' the streets might not be there continuously; sometimes they were in jail or institutions, and sometimes they did go home for a spell. Others were not 'of' the streets but lived with an unrelated person rather than their families. And what, he asks, about children who do resort to the streets regularly, but are somehow not in either category, such as child prostitutes and children running away from domestic service?

On this basis, Glauser prefers to think of 'street children' as 'the generic term used to refer to a group of children with a special relationship to the street'. Because this is contrasted to other children, with a different relationship to their families, he suggests that it is important to unpack the hidden assumptions in the way we use the words 'family', 'child', 'home' and 'street'.

'ON' THE STREET, OR 'OF' THE STREET?

... some of the boys who shine shoes at the central bus station of Asunción prefer working at night as long distance buses, leaving around midnight, means that an important number of passengers are waiting there in the early evening. Many of these may be potential customers. Also there is considerably less competition and therefore better business for the shoe shiners at night as there are fewer of them, since many parents do not allow their children out to work late at night. For others there are no late bus connections from home. Some of these children work all night whilst others get a few hours sleep wherever they can; some return home in the morning to get some sleep; others only go home every two or three days, spending the nights together with the children who do not go home on any regular basis at all (Glauser, 1990, p140).

Home, family and the street

At different times and in different places many family forms have existed and continue to exist, based on varied moral principles as well as a variety of relations between parents and children, husbands and wives. No single principle or structure of the family is needed for social life to carry on. It is simply necessary that society should make sure that the next generation receives adequate care so that the community continues into the future.

THE INTERNATIONAL VIEW IS THAT THERE IS ONLY ONE KIND OF FAMILY

The nuclear family is perceived to be the natural organisation of humans, while any other structures are labelled pathological. Most psychological and other professional literature supports this view (Tyler et al, 1992, p209).

Children can receive the care they need from a variety of blood relations and unrelated people in many different stuctures. When project workers talk about the children's families they are likely to be thinking about two biological parents. But the significant family reference point for children may be a mother or father alone, step- and god-parents, aunts and uncles, cousins, grandparents, or a sibling group – and they may make their home quite satisfactorily with any of these. Unfortunately, when some projects try to return street children to their 'families' they limit themselves to parents and don't explore the many viable alternatives.

The Unicef distinction assumes that when children are securely in families the home is 'the centre for play, culture and family life'. This shows a Northern experience of family life in private (and relatively spacious) dwellings, where the front door is shut against an apparently hostile world, and no experience whatsoever of family life in slums and shanty towns, where overcrowding forces play, culture and family life out on to the streets. For most of human history, socialisation and family relationships have taken place to a very large extent outside houses and, in urban areas, this means in the streets.

This is still the case for most poor communities. But the children playing on the streets within their own communities are not street children. The assumption hidden in the term 'street' in this context (even when it is 'in the widest sense of the word') is that it refers to spaces in the modern centres of cities. Fabio Dallape, who was the Director of the Undugu project in Nairobi for many years, has suggested that 'avenue' would be a better word than street. Avenues, boulevards, shopping malls, railway and bus stations are all modern spaces where children are not supposed to be out unaccompanied by an adult, and nobody is supposed to sleep Thus a street child is not just a child on any street but a child out of place, on thoroughfares that are intended for circulation of pedestrians and traffic.

AT HOME IN THE STREET

On the streets, home is a shop doorway, a bench in a square, a hot-air duct outside a restaurant, a bonfire on the beach, the steps of a railway station. Bed is a piece of cardboard, an old blanket, newspapers. Some sleep alone, others huddle together for warmth or protection. They never know when they might be woken up by a policeman's boot, a jet of cold water from a street-cleaning truck, or even a bullet from a vigilante group or a gun-happy officer of the law (Lusk, 1989).

What are street children really like?

There are many negative myths about street children (see pp13-14). What, then, is the reality?

STREET CHILDREN ARE NOT A DIFFERENT KIND OF CHILDREN

The situation of street children simply dramatises the more general condition of all children (Tyler et al, 1992, p207).

About their families

There has been little satisfactory research into the family backgrounds of street children. Most studies rely on poorly structured interviews with children and make no attempt to compare the samples with groups of children who are not on the street. Thus it is not possible either to confirm or deny any of the negative myths.

Most people who work with street children will agree that very few children have been abandoned. It is better to think of children gradually abandoning or breaking away from their families, and this happens for many reasons. Abusive and exploitative family relations may be involved, and these are sometimes associated with parental alcoholism or poor relationships with step-parents. Some children do come from mother-headed families, but many do not, and many more single mothers do not lose their children to the streets. The same is true of poverty. While lack of resources can make bad family relationships worse, there are many very poor families that stick together in spite of their circumstances. If that were not so, there would be many, many more children 'of' the street.

About their futures

The long-term outcomes of life on the streets as a child are simply not known. The one telling fact is that, in general, street adults have not been street children. Research in Mogadishu seems to show that being a street child is simply a stage in the life history of some people, who leave the streets once they become old enough to join the adult labour force. But it is likely that educational opportunities lost may mean being locked into a lifetime of unskilled, casual employment.

About the children themselves

More is known about the actual life of children on and of the streets and much of this denies the negative images. It is said that they are starving. The nutritional status of street children is not well documented but there is some evidence that, in certain circumstances, they may be better nourished than some of their contemporaries. Research in Nepal measured the nutritional status of rural children and compared this with three groups in Kathmandu: street children, school children and slum children. It was found that the rural children suffered from the greatest degree of malnutrition, followed by those from slums, streets and schools in that order. Researchers in South America have also noted that street children have better physical health overall, and are better nourished than their siblings at home.

One reason for this is that street children often have access to left-over food from restaurants, another that they earn and spend their own money. Children working on the street and returning home have to share their money with the whole family. In Jamaica it has been noted that some working children are in the habit of buying and eating fast food before they get home.

It is also said that they are thieves and that they have no choice but to be prostitutes. While some children may steal and prostitute themselves from time to time, this is not by any means their only means of survival. They have other opportunities for making money, such as car washing and minding, newspaper selling, street vending, ragpicking and scavenging, shoeshining, running errands and carrying bags, begging. Some children specialise; others jump from one opportunity to another, often in the same day. Although some do eventually specialise in stealing and prostitution, others want nothing to do with these activities, and still more only do them when they are forced to, either from necessity or because of coercion.

MAKING THE CHOICE IN JAMAICA

Street work in Jamaica is called 'hustling'. Parents had varied attitudes towards their children hustling by selling newspapers and wiping car windscreens. One household actually depended on the income, and at least one boy (aged 9) stated that his parents made him go out to hustle for the $5-6, which was the most he could make in the day. Another boy said that his father did not stop him hustling* because he was unemployed and 'mi can't depend on mi mother, so mi work to see what little mi can earn miself fi mi life'. Other parents stated that they would rather their boys did not hustle, but that the money was useful, and they seemed to have lost control of a situation in which the children had become to a very large extent autonomous.

The boys themselves seemed to make a distinction between 'working' and 'hustling', but could not be clear about defining each category. But they also made a distinction between hustling and criminal activities. As one boy stated, hustling is 'better for wi than wi go thief' (Ennew, 1982, p234).

---

* local term meaning getting money by any possible means

In addition, it is said that they are uncontrollably violent, have lost the ability to feel emotions such as love, have no morals and do not know how to play. Children living most of their lives on the streets do encounter violence on a daily basis, often at the hands of the police who are, after all, paid by society to keep the streets clean and safe. They also tend to experience violence from some older children and from psychologically disturbed street adults. Those who have experience of jails and detention centres almost always have scars to prove it. This all adds up to learning experiences that inevitably lead to fights between children. But this need not be irreversible. Lewis Aptekar records the surprise he and fellow researchers felt on their first visit to a project for street children in Cali, Colombia:

> Were the children as bad as we had been led to believe? We ran through our first impressions, noting all the healthy behaviour we had seen: the informal yet mannerly way in which the children ate, the kindness they showed to the sleeping children, the tolerance for those sucking their thumbs, the integration of the handicapped into their play, the lack of hostility and fighting in their crowded quarters, the brisk but orderly manner in which each child was allowed to get his own clothes, their quiet talks on the sidelines, and the way [one boy] was able to refrain from anger after being

punished in public. All of these were examples of healthy, nurturant behaviour and certainly not evidence of widespread conduct or personality disorders (Aptekar, 1988, p9).

This was not just a naive impression. Long-term research showed a far lower incidence of personality disorder than had been anticipated amongst street children.

In Johannesburg, Jill Swart has also found evidence that children living on the street hold surprisingly mainstream moral principles and she gives many examples of caring, altruistic behaviour among the children she works with (Swart, 1988, 1990). Similarly, a group of researchers comparing street children in Bogotá with street youth in Washington made the following observations:

> Overall, in spite of their hard lives, these street youth were amazingly less bitter than we had any reason to expect. They wanted to love and be loved, to have a role and to contribute. Their senses of the self, the world, and of how to negotiate their lives reflected their realities and the supports in them. They were aware of the threats and dangers, but not driven by them (Tyler et al, 1992, p206).

Many children living on the street speak about the importance of friendship in their lives and from around the world there are reports of the 'family groups' they form for mutual support.

AN EXAMPLE OF CARING BEHAVIOUR AMONG STREET CHILDREN

Setch (16) had both ankles broken when he was allegedly thrown from the first floor by police raiding the derelict building which was his home. For the six weeks during which his feet were encased in plaster, his five fellow *malunde** took it in turns to sit with him during the day. They provided food, comic books and pain-killers from the pharmacist for him (Swart, 1990, p74).

---

* local name for street child

No one who has ever watched street children for any length of time would miss the fact that they often break into spontaneous bursts of fun and recreation. It is often this engagingly playful behaviour that gets them photographed.

STREET CHILDREN ARE INDIVIDUALS

Our Bogotá interviews included 94 boys under age 18 who live on the streets. On the average, they were 13 and had left home at the age of 8. Most of them were first- and second-born sons, highly valued children in Colombian society. Many had been sexually or physically abused, shot, or stabbed. They lived by a combination of legal and illegal activities. They did not fit stereotypes of immature, greedy, self-centred, antisocial delinquents. Rather, many were responsible for someone else. When asked about home and institutions, they valued being cared for and having opportunities to contribute and/or to learn. They disliked abuse and betrayal. In fact, that is why they left their homes and institutions – they were not family or institutional rejects. When asked what they wished for, only 7 out of 258 wishes were antisocial or destructive. They wanted psychological supports, relationships, and a role in society. Less frequently, they wished for biological necessities, such as food and shelter.

The youths reported that, when not working, they enjoyed a wide range of activities, including destructive ones such as drinking and taking drugs. A substantial number were sexually active. *They were also children who made their own toys, played soccer and other games in the parks, splashed in the public fountains and slipped into the movies* (Tyler et al, 1992, pp203-4).

A final common view is that they are drug addicts and that many have Aids. Some street children do use cigarettes, alcohol and a variety of drugs. The latter are almost inevitably the cheapest available locally, which means solvents in many cases, but also marijuana and, in a few places, crack. Solvent abuse, in particular, causes volatile and unpredictable behaviour in users and this makes the street child solvent abuser very visible indeed at times. But they are not all users, or all addicted. In Honduras, for example, many street children resent the term 'resistoleros' applied indiscriminantly to all children on the street, whether or not they use the solvent 'resistol'.

DISCIPLINE AND DRUG USE IN NAIROBI

For street children, discipline and solidarity are closely linked in that discipline is necessary to protect their interest. Discipline is an important part of their lives. For example, the taking of drugs is limited to the amount required for action. Overdoses are not tolerated and street children force each other to moderation (Dallape, 1988, p18).

DRUG USE IN JOHANNESBURG

Some of the malunde exhibit symptoms of severe glue dependency ... Regular glue users commonly have hoarse voices and constantly running noses because the toluene in the glue they use attacks the respiratory system first. Impaired vision results from prolonged enlargement of the pupils and leads heavy users either to walk around with half-closed eyes as if squinting into the sun or to shun the daylight and live nocturnally. The skin on a child's head may take on a greyish pallor. The use of glue affects concentration and can cause rapid mood swings. Only two boys have been known to be quite unable to give up their glue; most are able to give it up for short periods while on the streets or permanently if taken into a setting where they are given sufficient warmth of caring and positive alternatives to street life (Swart, 1990, p89).

Street children are at risk of contracting sexually transmitted diseases, including HIV infection, when they have sex with infected adults for money or because of threats and violence. These infections also spread through communities of street children because some have sexual relations with each other. Both heterosexual and homosexual relationships are involved. HIV infection is not the most common sexually transmitted disease among street children, but it is the one that has attracted the greatest attention. In fact very little is actually known about the spread of HIV infection among street children. It is more than likely that they are particularly at risk of infection because:

- sex with an adult can lead to genital injuries and bleeding, so that the virus can be more easily transmitted;
- they may already have a history of sexually transmitted disease, which may increase their chances of HIV infection;
- their health may already be poor, meaning they are more vulnerable to infection;
- they do not have knowledge about HIV/Aids and do not know how to protect themselves;
- they cannot buy condoms, because they are children or because they cannot afford to;
- because they are children they do not have the power to insist that clients use condoms.

There are two additional problems for street children caused by the popular idea that they all have Aids. One is that the stigma can make discrimination against them even worse. The other is that some projects concentrate on this problem to the exclusion of all others. It is much more sensible to consider HIV as one health problem among many for street children.

STREET CHILDREN AND AIDS

... as more street children become infected with HIV, they may suffer even more discrimination. A doctor attending children in one of Brazil's largest state reformatories admitted: 'When a child tests HIV positive, I tell them "Prepare to die. You are going to die, you have Aids". We expel them. We cannot keep them here.' Not only is it cruel and misleading to tell a child with HIV that s/he is going to die (the child may remain healthy for many years), throwing them back on the street with a 'death sentence' and without ongoing support, is totally inhumane (Connolly, 1990, p1).

Working children

Working children do not have such a high profile as street children, so there are fewer myths to dispel. But before beginning to look at child workers it is worth repeating three important facts.

- Although they have specific problems, street children are a sub-set of working children. Even begging and stealing are work from the point of view of the child involved, because these are ways of getting enough money to survive.
- Over-concentration on street children hides the problems of larger groups of working children who are not so visible, nor so exciting, but whose problems are no less urgent. Child domestic workers may be even more alone and suffer from greater abuse. They certainly have less freedom. The nutritional status of children working in agriculture has been shown to be worse than that of street children. Youngsters working in factories and workshops suffer untold damage to their physical, psychological and intellectual development.
- Focusing on street children may divert scarce resources from these other at-risk groups, which is particularly important because street children projects tend to be very expensive in terms of the ratio of resources to the number of children who benefit.

What work do children do?
Children work in a variety of situations. Some work as helpers in family enterprises, helping on the family farm or assisting family members in agricultural labour, or

giving a hand in a small family-owned business such as a shop, street stall or workshop Most of these will be unpaid but be important to the family economy. Sometimes their help around the home, in childcare or household duties, will make it possible for an adult or older sibling to go out and earn a cash income. Other children work for wages themselves, usually in small unregistered businesses, or as casual labour in shops and restaurants.

Some children are self-employed in their own right, perhaps as shoeshiners, car washers or street vendors. Many of these, however, have to hand over some of their earnings to someone who supplies the goods – like newspaper vendors – or controls the pitch – as in the case of children who 'park' or wash cars and have to pay a premium to someone who controls the territory.

Finally, there are parts of the world in which children are sold by parents into bonded labour, often as pledge for a debt, or into apprenticeships, which are not always as benevolent as they may seem.

Types of work

Work is human activity, with social, physical, economic and personal aspects. It cannot be understood without taking into account who is working for whom and using what tools. It is part of the total relationship to the environment. It can bring positive socialisation and skill learning, or mean years of drudgery and boredom that limit the child's intelletual and educational potential, stunt physical and psychological growth and, under particularly hazardous conditions, can result in injury, illness and even death.

In the early 1980s, Gerry Rogers and Guy Standing made a list of the activities in which children are involved, in order to try to classify different types of work (Rogers and Standing, 1981):

- **Domestic:** Unpaid housework and childcare within the family.
- **Non-domestic, non-monetary:** Unpaid work with the family for the family's subsistence, or for sale.
- **Tied or bonded labour:** Some families lend out their children as workers in order to get a loan or pay a debt. Although this is forbidden by law, it is common in the Indian sub-continent and parts of South-East Asia and Latin America.
- **Wage labour:** Working for goods or money. Children may earn a wage alone or as part of a family group (for example on piece-work in plantations).
- **Marginal activities:** This is something of a catch-all category. It includes such varied occupations as street selling, manufacture in small workshops, ragpicking, begging, prostitution or stealing. The academic literature either refers to it as the 'informal sector' or the 'casual sector', but all academic work simply produces lists rather than analyses. Many working children

are in this category – if legislation forbids them to be employed as wage labourers and they still need an income, then they have very little choice.

- **Schooling:** Some people argue that school is work; certainly most children would agree. But what the theory claims is that this is economically important work because the children are acquiring the skills the nation needs them to have in the future. There are hidden costs to schooling, such as loss of potential earnings, the expense of uniforms, enrolment fees and books.

- **Idleness/unemployment:** Some children cannot go to school because of the hidden costs, and also cannot find work. Adults worry about children 'doing nothing', fearing that it will lead to mischief or worse. But it is worth remembering that activities that are worthless in an adult's eyes may be important for children.

- **Recreation and leisure:** Educationalists say that play is a child's work, a way of finding out about the world. Exercise and creative pursuits are essential for health at any age. Having fun with children is a good way of finding out about them and their problems, as many projects have discovered.

- **Reproductive:** No, Rogers and Standing are not talking about sex and parenthood! They mean the work that goes into keeping oneself going on a daily basis – getting clean, brushing teeth, washing clothes and so on.

Many children are involved in several activities on this list at the same time. Some manage to combine work, school and leisure. Others have a heavy burden of work in the home and outside. Then there is little time or energy left for school, let alone recreation. These tend to be the children whose welfare needs are greatest.

A CHILD'S WORK CAN BE HARD WORK: A JAMAICAN TEENAGE BOY'S ESSAY

When I am not in school I do a lot of things sometimes I go to taylor shop and do some pressing to get some money to come to school and when I am not pressing I am at the shoe make [maker's] shop and helping the shoemarke man fix shoes and the man gave me some money so i do all sort of job to hep myself to school because my mother cant afford to send me to school because she have a lot of small child and I am the fifth one and mi father isn't supporting we because he is not working so I have to work for myself, sometime I even go to sea but I dont like going there because it is too dreadful and too much fishermen die out there, but if you want to reach the top you have to come from the bottom, but I know that some day I am going To be something in life but I still enjoy what I do, and this is when I end my Composition (Ennew & Young, 1982, pp57-8).

Harmful work

Some child work is regarded as essential socialisation. For example, it is important for children in rural areas to learn agricultural skills. And learning how to do domestic tasks is equally vital. It is often assumed that work within the family or the home is non-hazardous, because parents will automatically protect their children. But it is difficult to draw the line, as in the following examples gathered during years of fieldwork:

- Mira is 13 years old. She stays home to look after three young brothers and do the cleaning and cooking while her mother works in the fields. She has never gone to school, because she will only need to learn household skills for her future life.

- Lucia has not yet been enrolled in school, despite being seven years old. As the eldest of three children she has to stay home and look after the babies while her mother goes to work in a factory. She finds the day very long, and the work hard. Last year she suffered severe burns when a pan was too heavy and she spilt scalding hot soup on her legs.

- When Benjamin gets home from school he has to start work washing dishes in the restaurant owned by his parents. It is nearly midnight when he has a chance to sit down and try to concentrate on his homework. Then he has to get up at 5.00 am to prepare the day's vegetables. As a result he has had to repeat Grade 2 three times. He doesn't like being a big ten-year-old in a class of seven-year-old children. Next year he thinks he will not bother with school.

- Shanthi works with her parents and brothers and sisters on a plantation. The whole family group has to work hard every day to fill baskets with balls of sap from rubber trees. Unless they fill ten baskets each day they will not be paid enough for them all to eat. The children are too tired to play and their mother has no energy to cuddle them. Quite apart from the work, they all suffer regularly from nausea and vomiting. The plantation is sprayed with chemicals and they have no protection. Shanthi's baby brother was born with a withered leg.

- Every spare moment that Sam has he works in his father's repair workshop He likes the work, but would also like to be able to play football with his schoolfriends from time to time. The problem is that his father sees this as 'wasting time'. If Sam is late back from school he is beaten. If his father has been drinking this really hurts, and Sam sometimes can't go to school because of the cuts and bruises.

Some families cannot or will not protect their children from the hazards of work, even in the home environment. This may be the result of poverty, of not knowing about children's development needs, of neglect or of abusive relationships. It is difficult to draw the line between child work and child labour, and many researchers and activists draw it in different places. There are also variations between societies, and sub-groups in societies, in the way people view children's work. This all causes as much confusion in its way as the distinction between children 'in' and 'of' the street.

The following principles are important to bear in mind when trying to decide between child work and child labour. Child labour is harmful. It threatens the child's physical, psychological, emotional and social development because:

- children are **too young** to be doing this kind of work;
- the hours are **too long**;
- children are **too small** for the tasks and tools involved;
- they are paid **too little**;
- the work is **too hard** for a small growing body;
- they have **too much** responsibility;
- the work is **too dull** and repetitive, and does not stimulate their development;
- the working environment is **too dangerous**: chemicals, excessive heat and noise, dangerous machinery are bad enough for adults, worse for developing bodies;
- they are **too unfree**: there has been no choice about whether or not to work, or what kind of work to do. They cannot leave. They lose their self esteem.

Legislation and working children

The responsibility for policing child labour lies at two levels: international intergovernmental bodies such as the United Nations, and national governments. In practical terms, the organisations that have often been most active in bringing the issue to public notice are non-governmental organisations, either in the human rights field or development aid agencies.

Most people would think of Unicef as the United Nations agency with the greatest interest in child work and street children. However, Unicef's main work has been the urgent issue of the health of children under five years of age. It has taken an interest in street and working children since 1985, but has mostly concentrated on programmes for street children, where it already has a track record. Unicef has a role in monitoring children's rights through the United Nations Convention on the Rights of the Child, but it is not responsible for legislation or for setting legal standards for child welfare.

The International Labour Office (ILO), which is a specialist agency of the United Nations dealing with workers' rights and is less well-known to the public than Unicef, has been trying to limit child work since 1919. The main international instrument is ILO Convention 138, adopted in 1973, which sets the legal minimum age for starting work at 15 years of age for most kinds of work. Unfortunately, very few countries have supported this measure. Fewer than 50 have committed themselves to making it part of their national laws.

CHILD LABOUR: THE ILO POSITION

The adoption of legislation specifying a minimum age of entry to employment, prohibiting child employment in certain occupations or activities, and regulating it where it is legally permitted has obvious and vital objectives. It helps establish certain labour norms and standards to which society can aspire and which can be used as a framework for policy, as well as providing a yardstick for evaluating performance and progress. Furthermore, it is one way of moving towards a common set of universal standards and ensuring that certain absolutes enshrined in international covenants and standards with regard to human dignity and human rights, including the rights of children, are observed and respected (Bequele & Boyden, 1988, p11).

Nevertheless, all societies have some sort of legislation about the age at which children should start work and the type of work they can do. Some have signed at least some of the ILO international conventions. Unfortunately child labour legislation is seldom enforced rigorously. This may be because:

- political will is lacking, and there are other, more pressing priorities;
- it is acknowleged that children have to work for survival;
- there are no resources available to police the law adequately;
- it is difficult to regulate marginal activities such as street vending;
- there is no central point of reference in government to deal with child work;
- compulsory school attendance is not enforced, schools are inadequate, teaching is poor, the curriculum is irrelevant, families do not see schooling as a priority;
- in some areas of the economy, child work is important (the export carpet industry for example);
- there are strong vested interests among employers to keep children working.

WHO IS RESPONSIBLE FOR ENFORCING CHILD LABOUR LAW?

Purely sectoral definitions of the problem lead to the absurdity in which police officials regard working children as a law enforcement problem, welfare agencies treat them as a social assistance problem, child rights advocates address them as a rights problem, educators view them as a school drop-out problem and so forth, while virtually nobody appreciates the problem as it is experienced by the impoverished youngsters who are at the centre of it all (Myers, 1991, p4).

Why employ children?
- Is it true that employers prefer child workers because their small hands can do some work faster than adults?

This assumption is often called the 'nimble fingers' argument. It is based on folk memories of small children being sent up chimneys or crawling between machines in spinning and weaving factories during the nineteenth century. It is suggested that in carpet weaving and electronics assembly child workers are necessary. They certainly are important, but in labour intensive industries this is for economic reasons rather than because of their supposed dexterity. Recent research has shown that, particularly in the case of younger children, lack of skill and stamina makes children less productive than adults. However, they are much cheaper to employ and cause few discipline problems.

Children do not join trades unions, are accustomed to obeying adults, can be paid less for doing the same job, know that they are working illegally and cannot complain to anyone.

THE REASONS FOR EMPLOYING CHILDREN

From an employer's point of view, child labour is perhaps the most stable form of labour; children do not strike or disrupt production. On the other hand, they are also the easiest to dislodge in times of economic difficulty. Children are the cheapest to hire and the easiest to fire. They do not resist. They are physically and emotionally vulnerable and are often physically and psychologically abused, or threatened with the possibility of such abuse (Bequele, 1991, p9).

THE NUMBERS GAME

One last word on preconceptions concerns the number of working and street children. As soon as you start thinking of working with this group, the question of numbers comes up; the global figures quoted by some agencies are enormous. Even before you begin work locally you will probably be contacted by a journalist interested in what you are doing, and the first question will be 'How many?' The media (particularly in the West) are obsessed with knowing the scale of any disaster or problem – how many dead? how many homeless? how many children are involved? – in any newsworthy situation. It is important to keep a level head on this one.

Neither Unicef nor the ILO can give any reliable or verifiable figures for the number of working children worldwide, including street children. A basic reason for the lack of accurate figures is that no one can agree on definitions. Nevertheless, some numbers are in circulation and have gained credibility. They are often cited at the beginning of reports and descriptions of street and working children, *but they have no validity or basis in fact.* There is a tendency for those who publicise children's difficulties to deal in huge numbers, in hundreds of millions, which are pure guesswork. Unfortunately, these are seldom questioned and often enter the official record, where they do become 'fact'.

It is possible to come up with a kind of instant demographic answer by using official figures and taking into account such factors as:

- percentage of total child population in each age group;
- children's participation in the workforce;
- enrolment in school, absenteeism, drop-out rates.

On such a basis, one estimate in the mid-1980s came to the conclusion that there were about 23 million working street children in developing countries (Ennew & Milne, 1989). But this is only instant demography and times have changed since the 1980s, bringing more of the world's children into urban poverty, including in former socialist countries.

An example of the absurdity of some of the figures being bandied about is the 100 million street children, which is among the numbers used at various times and in different contexts by Unicef and widely quoted by many writers. This figure was first dreamed up in the early 1980s and has not changed since, despite the constant assertion that the numbers of street children are rising inexorably. The ILO has the same problem with child labour figures.

There may be a case for knowing how many children are working on and off the streets worldwide, but it is more useful to know how many there are in your local area, to use proper research to find out about their situation and to

devise good interventions that will really help them. It may suit the ↑
to be able to deal in shocking figures of hundreds of millions, but th
children rather than helping them. In the last analysis, even one tired, un
working child is one too many.

THE BEST RESOURCE IS THE CHILDREN

As we have already seen, the Western model of childhood tends to emphasise children's need for protection and the requirement to provide for their emotional, physical and intellectual development. This means that they are not seen as responsible and are seldom asked for their opinions. It is assumed that they would make mistakes and not understand the situation. Children should be 'seen but not heard'. We ask their parents and teachers to tell us what their problems are, and what the solutions should be. We don't ask them.

Children who work to support themselves and their families, or who live away from adult supervision, *are* responsible. In many societies they are expected to do things for themselves and others at far younger ages than would be expected in developed countries. It is only logical that they will have views about this and that they should be involved in plans to help them.

Richard Hart has made a particular study of children's participation and developed a 'ladder of participation' to show the ways in which adults involve children (or fail to do so) (Hart, 1992).

Hart points out that there are many examples of children being able to organise themselves without being helped by adults, and suggests that we try to remember making and carrying out projects that were secret from adults during our own childhoods:

> Such examples from your own memory are the most powerful evidence of young people's competence. The principle behind such involvement is motivation; young people can design and manage complex projects together if they feel some sense of ownership in them. If young people do not at least partially design the goals of the projects themselves they are unlikely to demonstrate the great competence they possess. Involvement fosters motivation, which fosters competence, which in turn fosters motivation for further projects (Hart, 1992, p5).

Of course, children participate in projects just by being in them, but this does not mean that their views are taken into consideration or that they can affect the way the project is run. Even projects that say children participate in this way may have

The Ladder of Participation

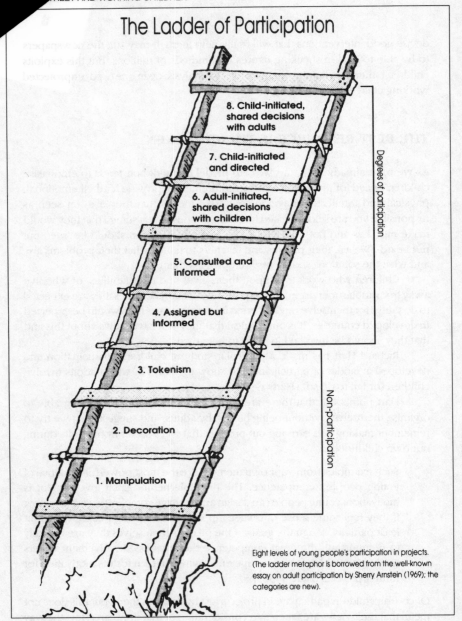

8. Child-initiated, shared decisions with adults

7. Child-initiated and directed

6. Adult-initiated, shared decisions with children

5. Consulted and informed

4. Assigned but informed

3. Tokenism

2. Decoration

1. Manipulation

Degrees of participation

Non-participation

Eight levels of young people's participation in projects. (The ladder metaphor is borrowed from the well-known essay on adult participation by Sherry Arnstein (1969): the categories are new).

Source: Innocenti Essays No. 4: Children's Participation, 1992; Unicef International Child Development Centre, Spedale degli Innocenti, Florence, Italy.

a mistaken idea of what participation means.

In the context of projects:

- 'participation' means that children are encouraged and facilitated to analyse their situation, decide what the priority problems are and suggest solutions. They will also be actively involved in the day-to-day running of the project;
- 'participation' does not mean children being involved in public activities of the project: singing songs they have been taught by adults and carrying banners with slogans written by adults; children being exposed to public display to tell their stories; consulting children about project choices that have been drawn up by adults.

Of course, real participation, in which children initiate project options and share decisions with adults, is not easy. It does not happen overnight and children cannot make choices without knowing what the choices are, their possible outcomes and how to make decisions democratically. Although they already have much knowledge and many skills they still need more information and further social skills in order to be able to participate. The adult role is to facilitate their participation, giving them the tools to do the job and supporting their efforts.

In practice, relying on children's competence is increasingly proving to be a vital component of project planning. For example, in Bogotá:

> The competency framework has provided us a basis for changing to a primary prevention orientation. By using it, we were able to involve kids and street workers with us in defining themselves and their world. We all became part of the solution instead of different aspects of the problem (Tyler et al, 1992, pp206-7).

The most important resource in project design and management is not money, or buildings, or adult skills, but the children themselves. They are not 'objects of concern' but people. They are vulnerable but not incapable. They need respect, not pity. True child participation should be the goal of every project and a constant consideration of project management and workers alike.

WHO KNOWS MOST ABOUT CHILDREN?

... the children themselves are the experts: they know what their concerns are and how they see their own future (Connolly, 1990a, p10).

QUESTIONS TO ASK

Of yourself

- What do you think childhood should be like?
- What sort of work should children do, and at what ages?
- What is your image of street children?
- What do 'home' and 'street' mean to you?
- What work is bad for children – and why?
- Why are children employed rather than adults?
- What experiences of organisation did you have as a child? How much did this depend on adult help and advice?

About the children you will work with

- What is childhood like for poor children in the area where you want to start a programme?
- What is the local image of street children?
- Might the distinction between children 'on' the street and children 'of' the street make sense for the children you want to work with?
- What facts do you have about the children you want to work with? What are these based on?

About the area where you will start a project

- What do 'home' and 'street' mean to people in this area?
- What work do children do?
- What are the numbers that are publicly available for street children and/or child workers?
- Are there any examples of child participation in programmes and projects locally? What kind of participation is involved?

Chapter 3

RESEARCH USING EXISTING INFORMATION

Projects with street and working children must be grounded in local reality.

There is an obvious sense in which all street children are alike. They live and work on the streets and, like adults who do the same, they experience similar environmental hazards: traffic, police, lack of shelter and privacy, lack of sanitation. These lead to a similar set of outcomes – accidents, beatings, prison, exposure to the elements, feelings of being left out of society, disease. But they live on different streets, within different cultures and no two cities are the same.

Children who work away from the streets also share certain characteristics. They are poorly paid compared to adults and their working conditions may be more hazardous, they are less likely to be protected by employment legislation and their education and development will be affected. But no two industries and no two countries are identical.

WHAT IS ALREADY KNOWN?

Street and working children are part of the general child population and their situation is rooted in the overall national situation, which includes political, economic and social life as well as cultural ideas about families and children. Although hard facts about street and working children are likely to be difficult to come by and the information is inevitably incomplete, it is important to start with what is known and gather basic information before you start carrying out your own research.

Information will be available from three main sources, the government, the local community of NGOs, and international organisations. You need to know about:

- legislation affecting children;
- the child population as a whole, and about particular at-risk groups;
- government policies for and affecting children;
- the employment and unemployment situation for adults;
- economic and social factors affecting children;

- family structures and the position of women;
- the education system;
- child health;
- attitudes towards street and working children;
- policies, programmes and services for street and working children.

The limited information available is overwhelmingly concerned with two age groups, children under five years old and young people over the age of 15. The first concentrates on health aspects, and the second on employment/unemployment and problem areas such as delinquency, sexuality and drug use.

WHAT DO WE KNOW ABOUT CHILDREN?

... if the principle of protecting the most vulnerable is to be taken seriously, then it must be a process which can be monitored and measured. And the fact is that whereas most nations can and do produce up-to-date quarterly statistics on the health of their economies, few nations can produce even annual statistics on the health of their children. This failure to monitor the effects of economic and social changes on the most vulnerable, and particularly on the growing minds and bodies of young children is both a cause and a symptom of the lack of political priority afforded to this task. Yet there could be no more important test for any government than the test of whether or not it is protecting the nation's vulnerable and whether or not it is protecting the nation's future – and its children are both.

Today, the indicators for measuring the performance of that duty – the quarterly measurement of, for example, changes in child nutrition, immunisation coverage, and the prevalence of low birth weights – are not even in place. Indeed we know far more about changes in the weather or in viewing figures for television shows, or in consumer preferences and the monthly sales of video recorders, than we do about changes in the nutritional health of the under-fives (Unicef, 1987, *State of the World's Children, 1988*, pp30-1).

Children of school age do not present the same degree of health problems as the vulnerable under-fives and have not yet come to be seen as a threat to society as have out-of-control youth. Although it is important to consider the older age group in planning projects, it is between the ages of five and 15 that many children begin to be economically active and perhaps start a relationship with the street that may lead to them making it their home.

Most of the information we have about this age group consists of statistics on schools. What children do when they are *not* in school, and the relationships between their work and the education system, are usually virtually empty boxes in information terms. Some of the information does exist, but needs to be collected together to form a general background. Some you will have to find out for yourself.

OUT OF SCHOOL, ON THE STREETS, AT RISK

Pedro, 11 years old, told us his daily routine when we talked to him: 'In the morning I go to the market to guard cars, in the afternoon I go to school. After class I watch cars at Dixie's and at night at Barrabar's.' Pedro must take money home; otherwise his parents accuse him of having been lazy or losing the money gambling. To avoid unpleasant moments, he prefers not to go home when he has no money. His parents worry about him, about his delays and absence, as well as the irregularity with which he attends school. It seems however that no one in his family – in this case, an economically more stable family than others – knows how to respond to him (*Working in the streets*, p103).

WHERE IS THE INFORMATION?

All countries collect information about children, although this is never as complete as it might be. It is often scattered around different ministries and other government agencies. This chapter deals with some of the ways of gathering the material already available, to provide a base showing what is known and where the gaps in information are. Once that is established you should be able to formulate some research questions of your own.

Much of this work involves making contacts with a variety of groups and will be involved in later stages of the work. A list of contact addresses for international organisations mentioned is given at the back of this manual.

International sources

Over the past ten years or so children have taken a higher profile in national and international policies, to a certain extent because of interest in the United Nations *Convention on the Rights of the Child.* You need a copy of the Convention. The most important article for working children is Article 32, which deals with economic exploitation, but articles about health, welfare, justice, education and families also have implications for street and working children. And do not forget Articles 12 and 15, which are about children's participation in society.

ARTICLE 32

1. States Parties recognise the right of the child to be protected from economic exploitation and from performing any work that is likely to be hazardous or to interfere with the child's education, or to be harmful to the child's health or physical, mental, spiritual, moral or social development.
2. States Parties shall take legislative, administrative, social and educational measures to ensure the implementation of this article. To this end, and having regard to the relevant provisions of other international instruments, States Parties shall in particular:
(a) provide for a minimum age or minimum ages for admissions to employment;
(b) provide for appropriate regulation of the hours and conditions of employment; and
(c) provide for appropriate penalties or other sanctions to ensure the effective enforcement of this article.

ARTICLE 12

1. States Parties shall assure to the child who is capable of forming his or her own views the right to express those views freely in all matters affecting the child, the views of the child being given due weight in accordance with the age and maturity of the child.
2. For this purpose, the child shall in particular be provided the opportunity to be heard in any judicial and administrative proceedings affecting the child, either directly, or through a representative or an appropriate body, in a manner consistent with the procedural rules of national law.

Most nations have signed and ratified the Convention, becoming 'States Parties', which means that they are obliged to produce country reports on children's rights for the monitoring Committee. Some have already been submitted and many more are in the pipeline. They are of varying quality but nevertheless provide important baseline information (sometimes as much for what is missing as what they contain). If you cannot get hold of a copy in-country, write to the **Commission on Human Rights** in Geneva. In some cases non-governmental organisations have produced 'alternative reports', which should also be available from the Commission.

Many countries have been assisted in writing their reports by the local Unicef office, which may have carried out a national *Situational Analysis of Women and Children* (sometimes virtually indistinguishable from the country report). Although Unicef tends to concentrate on infant and young child survival and maternal and child health, this will still be a useful document. Many Unicef offices have also carried out situational analyses for what the organisation calls 'children in especially difficult circumstances'. This is a ragbag of a category that is under review, but it includes street and working children. These reports may not be published and are of extremely varied quality, but it is worth asking for a copy. Quite apart from the information they contain, they can give useful leads to local organisations and researchers.

ARTICLE 44 OF THE CONVENTION ON THE RIGHTS OF THE CHILD

1. States Parties undertake to submit to the Committee, through the Secretary General of the United Nations, reports on the measures they have adopted which give effect to the rights recognised herein and on the progress made on the enjoyment of those rights:
(a) within two years of the entry into force of the Convention for the State Party concerned,
(b) thereafter every five years.
2. Reports made under this article shall indicate factors and difficulties, if any, affecting the degree of fulfilment of the obligations under the present Convention. Reports shall also contain sufficient information to provide the Committee with a comprehensive understanding of the implementation of the Convention in the country concerned ...
6. States Parties shall make their reports widely available to the public in their own countries.

The **International Labour Office** (ILO) has publications (including manuals), country reports and country programmes for child workers (including street children). It is worth being in contact both with the child labour specialists at the headquarters in Geneva and with the country representative.

It is also worth contacting **Defence for Children International** (DCI) at the International Secretariat in Geneva, which will be able to put you in contact with the local DCI section, if there is one. This should bring you into contact with local people who are active in children's rights, who may have carried out their own surveys and could be useful in the following situations:

- in the early stages by guiding you through important issues in the maze of national laws affecting children;
- later on in advocacy work for individual children and the group of children you eventually decide to work with.

CHILDREN'S 'RIGHTS' IN EMPLOYMENT

The employment of minors has advantages for employers for several reasons: their income is significantly lower than the minimum wage for adults, the employers do not have to make contributions to social security, children can be easily fired, and they cannot set up trade unions. In general terms, it can be said that minors are not only the least-protected labour sector, but also the most exploited. The problem goes beyond the mere infringement of the law: because these minors have a pressing need to work they eagerly take on any remunerated activity even though the pay may be inadequate for the effort and hours required. The situation is made worse by the fact that no organisation exists to defend their interests and rights and to register complaints of maltreatment.

(From an account of Defence for Children International, Third Latin American Meeting, December 1991)

Another source of useful contacts is **Childwatch International**, which has a worldwide database of individuals and institutes researching children's issues. In addition, there are regional networks of organisations working with street children and child labourers, which are sources of information, contacts and support (see both the address list in Appendix 4 and *Street and working children: a resource file*, see Appendix 3).

National and local government sources

For a situation analysis for the entire child population you could gather most of what you need to know from ministries dealing with families, health and education. For street and working children you need to throw the net wider and be more innovative.

Local legislation

In many countries the main outlines of what childhood should be like are written in a specific legal code for children or minors, or in laws for family life. Other countries do not have such special legislation. In all cases, laws affecting children can be found in many different parts of the legal system. Legislation on education, housing and public health affects all children. Other legal influences on their lives include laws:

On family life
- The position of women
- Marriage and divorce

- Registration of births and deaths
- Adoption
- Social security and other welfare systems
- Legitimacy

A SURVEY OF GOVERNMENT INFORMATION ON CHILD LABOUR IN MALAYSIA

The collection of this information on children's work is confined to participation in wage labour, and little or no recognition is made of the fact that most of the work children do takes place outside. Also, the purpose of the data collected by these agencies is to estimate other aspects, like labour force and education participation, and not to actually look at children's labour as such. For the purpose of this study ... the main sources of data used are:
(i) The 1980 Population Census for data on the employment of the 10-14 age group
(ii) Education statistics on enrolment and drop-outs from 1980 through 1988.
(iii) Welfare statistics for girls under 15 years of age found in the company of prostitutes or working at bars.
(iv) Health statistics for children under 12 years of age who were either outpatients or inpatients at the General Hospital for 'accidents caused by machinery' and 'accidents caused by cutting and piercing instruments'.
(v) Labour statistics for the number of employees found violating the *Children and Young Person's (Employment) Act 1966* (George, 1992, p9).

On employment
- Minimum ages for different types of work
- Conditions of work, including factory inspection
- Street vending
- Prostitution
- Betting, lotteries and gaming

On law and order
- Public order and right of assembly
- Justice, and juvenile justice in particular
- Prisons, punishment and detention of juvenile offenders in particular
- Alcohol and drug use
- Pornography

Laws affecting particular groups of children
- Refugees and asylum-seekers
- Ethnicity, race, indigenous groups and other discriminations
- Immigration
- Military service

This may seem like a very long list, but it is intended to get you thinking rather than acting as a shopping list for all the legal documents you need to get hold of. Local conditions and common sense will dictate clear priorities.

Official information

Governments not only collect and publish information about children, but different government departments and agencies carry out research. This may be at national, regional and local levels. It is worthwhile investigating the information available from the following sources:

- **Population and Census Departments**. Of particular interest here are figures on child deaths and illness, especially for the age group 5-15 years, and looking especially for signs of any that may be work-related. These might be accidents and 'traumatic' injuries (which could include amputations or eye injury, for example), child homicides or illness related to the working environment (respiratory problems, perhaps). These figures will be too global to give precise facts, but they may indicate fruitful areas for further investigation. Differences by gender, region and ethnic group are worth noting. Quite apart from other considerations, it is useful to have some overall figures for the child population as a whole that can serve as baseline data.

- **Ministry of Health**. The Ministry may have more detailed information than the census office on deaths and illnesses. Hospital and primary health care services may also have useful records, particularly admission data and medical histories. Don't forget to check the information on treatment for sexually transmitted diseases.

- **Ministry of Education**. School enrolment, attendance and drop-out figures can be very revealing, as can data on repetition of grades. Often the best sources for this are local schools. It is particularly important to look for differences by gender, region, ethnic group Seasonal differences and variations between different school shifts may also indicate child work that interferes with schooling. Teachers can be wonderful sources of information. It is also important to look at the school system as a whole. How relevant is the curriculum to the lives of children from poor families? Do they learn skills that are going to be useful in getting employment? What are the hidden costs of school attendance (enrolment fees, books, uniforms)? Is it difficult for children to get to schools, especially secondary schools? Are the schools well equipped? What methods of teaching are used? What is teacher training like? What are the relationships between parents and teachers and children and teachers? Do schools provide any benefits, such as free meals? Are there any special education services for children with learning difficulties or disabilities? If so, how accessible and appropriate are they? Most of the answers to these questions are likely to be negative, but this is still baseline information.

- **Ministry of Employment/Labour**. Background information about the principal sources of employment for adults, industries, wages, unemployment and under-employment figures (by age, gender and region). Many ministries of employment carry out studies of what is usually called the 'informal sector', which does not always appear in official employment statistics. As child labour in formal, waged employment is usually forbidden by law, most children work in the 'informal sector' and it is useful to have some idea about the local informal work scene. Unfortunately, most ministry studies only look at the more organised parts of the sector – such as regular street trading or small workshops – and do not take into account the really casual work that is often done by children such as wandering street traders, shoeshiners or newspaper vendors. But official information will give plenty of information about the working lives of parents in poor communities. Some official sources, especially municipal authorities, do carry out studies of child workers and street children. Factory inspectorate records can be revealing, especially if they include prosecutions for illegal use of child labour.

- **Justice and Police Departments**
  Juvenile justice records
  Police records (especially at the local station)
  Court records
  Probation and detention statistics
  Information about prostitution
  Prosecutions and detentions for vagrancy
  Drug and alcohol use

- **Ministry of Welfare/The Family and Children**
  Numbers of children in state care or without families
  Child abuse and neglect figures
  Family structure and family size statistics and studies
  Studies of 'children at risk', 'irregular families', etc.

A note on access

It is inevitable that many of these data sets will not exist, or will not be made available to you. Many countries have neither the resources nor the inclination to collect some of these items. Sometimes the information will exist, but the terminology will be different. It is important to learn the official langauge used in work on children and families, because this differs from country to country Sometimes the information will be poor because of bad data collection methods, inadequate analysis or inept presentation.

Official reports and research documents may be gathering dust on a shelf somewhere, so it is really worthwhile making good contacts and trying to get access to the shelves. Bureaucrats often don't know what they have stored away, or may not understand the importance of certain kinds of information for your purposes. Don't just ask if they have a report on child labour or street children; make sure they understand that you are looking for information on children for general background purposes, and hope you will be let loose on the archives. To say you are looking for background material on child welfare is far less threatening than asking about sensitive issues such as street children and child labour.

Academic sources

There are several possible sources of information in the academic world, and it is important to check all of them:

- Unicef and government reports are often commissioned from local researchers in universities and institutes of higher education. There is usually a pool of experts on children's issues you can contact. Their skills may be variable, but it is important to know who the local experts are.
- The most useful academic contacts will be with psychology departments, schools of education and social work, sociology and anthropology departments. Schools of medicine and public health are also helpful.
- Further information will probably exist in student dissertations and theses. Welfare-oriented MA, PhD and undergraduate students in all the disciplines mentioned often write their theses on child workers and street children, and these can contain extremely useful information. A word of warning: it is usually not productive to ask Heads of Department if there are any theses of this type available, copies will be deposited in libraries and it will be necessary to spend staff time looking for them. But it's worth the trouble.

Non-governmental organisations

There are three reasons for contacting non-governmental organisations in the course of preliminary information gathering:

- They may have information and research reports of their own.
- You need to know what projects and resources for street and working children already exist.

- In some cases, the official country report to the Committee on the Rights of the Child has been accompanied by an 'alternative' NGO report. For example, Save the Children was instrumental in the alternative report made by NGOs in Honduras, and is working with coalitions of NGOs in several other countries.

ANALYSING THE INFORMATION COLLECTED

Validity

First you need to assess the validity of the material you have gathered, looking particularly for contradictions between data sets from different sources. These may be due to differences of definition, or perspective, or to different methods of data collection. You should think about what were the underlying assumptions about families, children, working children and street children made by the researchers, and identify particular groups of children, particular places, certain industries that seem to give rise to anxiety. You need to consider whether this is justified, or just a reflection of prevailing political, social or cultural concerns (a guide to this is whether or not the media are taking an interest).

Some groups of working children may not be studied. You should find out the reasons for this. Finally, you should decide which groups of children you think are most at risk, and of what.

A picture of what is known

Any of these sources, particularly at regional and local levels, may have programmes, policies and projects for street and working children. Knowing about these is vital if you are to avoid reinventing the wheel and duplicating some other agency's efforts. You can begin by noting what is actually known about:
- the situation of children in general, and of street and working children in particular;
- the problems faced by poor families, in terms of housing, employment, food security, income, health, and family relationships;
- the extent to which children are working rather than going to school, and the effects on their development;
- where children work, what work they do, which children work (are any groups particularly at risk?);
- the official and public views of 'the family', 'the child', child work and street children;

- what hazards are faced by specific groups of working children (injury and illness, psychological damage, intellectual and phsyical impairment, behavioural problems).

You can then make a list of all the plans, projects and developments that already exist to help street and working children, either directly or indirectly. This will enable you to identify what you think might be the gaps between what children need and what is done to meet their needs.

At the end of this process you should have some idea about four things:

- Which groups of children are most at risk.
- Which groups of these children are receiving least help.
- Which of these groups you might best be able to help.
- What further information you will need about these children in order to start the project planning process.

WHY GATHER INFORMATION?

The need to know more about the situation, characteristics, feelings and problems in the everyday life of street children arose from an increasing urge to take action on their behalf (Glauser, 1990, p138).

QUESTIONS TO ASK YOURSELF

- Have you checked what information is available from Unicef, the ILO and international NGOs working locally?
- Have you collected information about children from national and local government sources, including copies of relevant legislation?
- Have you made contact with local education, health and legal authorities, including contacts with schools, hospitals, clinics, welfare departments and police, to collect any information that seems relevant?
- Have you made contact with local projects working with children, and asked if you can see their reports?
- Have you found out the names of interested academics, and obtained copies of reports and theses?
- Have you made time to study all the information, decided where the gaps are and what more you need to know?

Chapter 4

CARRYING OUT YOUR OWN
FIRST HAND RESEARCH

Your own first hand research is the next step It provides a baseline for future monitoring as well as sound reasons for taking decisions about which children to help and why. It has two elements:
- What local people bring to the situation in terms of ideas and attitudes.
- The information you need in order to plan, implement and evaluate your project.

Local people may mean different things when they talk about children, work, family and community. There will probably be differing attitudes among different groups. Wealthier, westernised professionals may well have much the same ideas as you. Families who see children as an important investment in the present and future welfare of their group may see things differently. They may be more likely to see children as capable and responsible at earlier ages and less likely to value education as an option for its own sake.

Some of the research techniques outlined in this chapter should help establish what these ideas are for the local community. Unless a project addresses local ideas it cannot be successful.

Last, but very much not least, you need to know what the children think. This is not window-dressing, it is crucial that you take their views seriously at all times.

Your research into already existing information will have thrown up as many questions as answers. It will have provided a lot of background data, but it will also have revealed gaps in information and made you want to know more about certain aspects. You should have some idea about which group or groups of children you now wish to target, and finding out more about them is the motive for doing your own research in order to base your project on sound information.

Is your own research really necessary?

Some people claim that there is no time for new research, that we know enough already and that the important thing is to act for disadvantaged children *immediately*. These people usually want to rescue children and often quote from a poem by Nobel laureate Gabriela Mistral: 'Many things can wait. Children cannot. To them we cannot say tomorrow, their name is today.' The answer to this is not just that 'fools rush in', but also that we cannot afford to say to children 'Sorry, I didn't take time to get it right yesterday; I'll try again tomorrow.'

Research need not be long, complicated and academic. When it is connected to work with children it should be related solely to their concerns and interests and to action on their behalf in ways they think is appropriate. Unfortunately, this is rarely the case, and for this reason research and researchers have a poor reputation with activists. But research is necessary. Children deserve professional, responsible help based on verifiable facts. Amateurism is just not good enough, however well-meaning. The organisers of a pilot project in Manila found that 'a few carefully conducted studies at the beginning save time and money by focusing efforts on the main problems' and also provided hard facts that convinced officials and parents alike that long-term action was essential (Gunn & Ostos, 1992, p643).

Moreover, as Benno Glauser points out, it is not acceptable 'that international organisations, policy-makers, social institutions and individuals who feel entitled to intervene in the lives of children with problems should do so on the basis of obviously unclear and arbitrary knowledge about the reality of these children's lives' (Glauser, 1990, p144).

Research for its own sake has no value in a project setting. But research that is focused on precise project planning, implementation and evaluation is vital. With this approach, the research process need be neither prolonged nor expensive. The following ground rules will help to cut out unnecessary work:

- It is important to concentrate on the things you really need to know in order to make an effective intervention, and monitor its effectiveness regularly.
- Avoid the tendency to ask too many questions just because other researchers have done so.

THE RESEARCH PROCESS

Project staff and outside researchers

Over the years, social researchers have developed a bad name for themselves. Many project workers will have had the experience of spending weeks helping an earnest PhD student interview parents and children involved in their project, making sure that the right number of questionnaires from the correct sample of people are filled in. Then the researcher takes the pile of survey forms back to the university and that is the last the project sees of her – project workers probably don't even get to see a copy of the thesis. In any case, they suspect, from discussions they had with the student, that she didn't understand the situation. Many of the questions on her schedule were not relevant to the children they work with every day, whose lives may be almost as familiar to them as their own.

Even when the researcher is not a student, but an expert sociologist or psychologist, the situation may not be very different. Project workers and academics often fail to understand each other's points of view. They simply don't share enough information prior to beginning research. So the academic may spend weeks, even months, on the project, gathering data without much discussion and then write up the data into a report that seems remote from the project's realities.

Nevertheless, it *is* important to have an outside view. It is so easy sometimes to miss what is under your nose, or to exaggerate one aspect of children's lives simply because it seems to you to be a priority. Often what appears to be most important to a project worker is some aspect that he or she finds shocking and difficult to deal with, so this theme comes to the forefront. However, this can also be true of researchers!

SURVEYS OF CHILDREN: VIEW FROM A PROJECT

Some people start their contact with street children through a survey. Making a survey in order to assess the number of children, their background, the areas where they come from, the difficulties they experience, etc. Usually they employ people from universities who are in a position to prepare good questionnaires and approach donor agencies for funds ...

The children don't believe in those surveys, because they have been approached by so many students and people and police who have questioned them about their street life. We don't believe in such external surveys either, since we already know the answers to most of the questions we put in the questionnaire ...

The children, fortunately, don't take a survey seriously and so don't have false expectations. Children don't care to answer survey questions correctly. In fact they rarely give correct answers to your questions whether you are a foreigner or a local ... They enjoy elaborating on the hardship of their life and how they must survive. They want to impress you, they act like actors in a theatre ...

Make a survey with them about themselves and their areas of origin ... The survey must be prepared beforehand with them: they must all know the type of information you need. They should even be aware of the reasons for such a survey ... Organise a seminar to discuss the findings with them (Dallape, 1988, pp24 and 28).

Collaboration is the name of the game at all stages of research, collaboration between research worker and project staff (and other participants, including children, as the work develops). Project managers must always be in control of the research process in the sense of knowing what they want to get out of it and why, which must be directly related to project planning and evaluation. Managers should be part of the research process. It is just not enough to ask an academic to find out about the children's lives and then sit back and wait for the results. Managers and researchers need to agree on questions such as: Which children? Why? In what depth? What aspects?

It is unwise to accept the research proposal of an outside researcher carrying out research for another purpose and hope that the results will be useful for the project. In other words, both project staff and outside researchers must spend some time developing and agreeing on terms of reference that are relevant to the research task in hand. The bottom line is:

- What questions does the project want to ask about a particular group of children at any one time?
- How should these questions be asked (what methods are the most appropriate in practical and ethical terms)?
- How is this related to project objectives, goals and future actions?
- Who else may need to know the results (including the children)?

CONSULTING EXPERTS IN THE SMOKEY MOUNTAIN PROJECT

Until the Community Workers began to observe and record cases of accident, injury and psychological trauma among the child workers, no one had realised just how numerous they were. To determine which additional health services the children should have, a detailed occupational health study was undertaken by the project, in conjunction with the School of Public Health, University of The Philippines ... The research consisted of air, water and soil sampling from the site, an extensive battery of medical examinations on a sample of 235 Drop-in Center children, dietary analyses, and a KAP (health knowledge, attitude, practice) study of these children and their families (Gunn & Ostos, p638).

There are several reasons why an outside researcher may be useful at different stages of a project:

- To help design suitable research methodology with the project workers.
- To help project workers carry out the research and analyse the results.

- To help establish the viability and credibility of the project.
- To carry out periodic external evaluations in collaboration with staff and participants.
- To use specific technical expertise to answer particular research questions that have arisen in the course of project development.

Special issues in research with children

Surprisingly few social scientists have studied children, let alone street and working children. When they do research children's lives they usually agree that there are certain questions that make this work different from researching adults. These questions are in fact relevant in research with adults, but the way we define children as incapable focuses our attention on particular problems as if they were unique to childhood. The questions are:

- Should I research them?
- Will they talk to me?
- Will they tell the truth?

Should I research children?

This question is not the most common to be asked by researchers, but it is gaining importance because of the Convention on the Rights of the Child. It is related to children's legal status in society and their lack of power compared to adults. It has become common practice for researchers to ask adult research subjects for permission to carry out the research. This is referred to as 'informed consent' because the subjects are supposed to understand the purpose of the research, know what the research process will entail and be guaranteed confidentiality or anonymity in research reports.

In theory children cannot give consent in law, but the Convention provides them with the right to have their opinions respected. In most research with children permission is given by parents or legal guardians. Sometimes children are not consulted at all, but this is increasingly regarded as unacceptable.

In the case of street children it may be impossible to obtain formal permission from parents. It would clearly be equally unacceptable to use the fact that parents cannot be contacted as a reason not to carry out research that might help to improve children's lives.

The best option, whether or not parents have been contacted for formal consent, is to negotiate research permission with the children. This is unlikely to be as easy to do as it is to write. But it should be a guiding principle of research, and under constant review. The more vulnerable a child is, the greater the responsibility of researchers and project workers to respect his or her views and opinions.

Children are powerless compared to adults. Thus, even if they are asked for consent, it can be argued that they are unlikely to withhold it because researchers and project workers are not only adults but richer, better educated and often from an obviously more important social group An adult, white, male, middle-class researcher will usually have no difficulty obtaining consent to the research process from a poor, black, female child.

Children who are working, especially those who are living on the streets, are actually less likely in many cases to be cowed into submission by adult researchers. Street children can vote with their feet, and many would-be researchers have reported their research subjects simply running away. The point is that they have a right to do so!

CHILDREN'S REACTIONS TO BEING RESEARCHED: URBAN INDIA

Many of the [street] children in our study expressed concern regarding the actual benefits this study would bring them. Their wariness of the promises made to them by so many people in the past and their lack of faith in the government was revealed by statements such as:

- 'How will this study help us?'
- 'So many people have come and talked to us. But what have they done for us?'
- 'What has the government done for us?'

... The children were also aware of the movie by Mira Nair, *Salaam Bombay*, that was supposed to have exposed to the Indian people and their government, their problems, particularly those faced by their fellow street child, Shafiq (who was originally from Bangalore ...), the star of the movie. The children expressed their anger that, in spite of all this, nothing was done about their problems (Reddy, 1992, p14).

They may also run away because they have had good reason to be afraid of adults. Jill Swart in Johannesburg found that black street boys ran from her, a middle-class white woman, because they thought she was approaching them for sex (Swart, 1988, p14). Other street children may fear being taken to reformatories, adult prisons or police cells. In several countries children have experience of violence, and the death of their friends, at the hands of police and public. These are all sensitivities that must be taken into consideration in the ethical question of informed consent.

RESPECT THE CHILDREN

There were some hard lessons the children forced us to learn. We had no right, they asserted, to keep on questioning them, if we could and would do nothing for them. Too many people had done this before; written articles, filmed interviews and got their names in the papers, but where were they now? (Reddy, 1992, Preface).

A further ethical issue is the effect on children of publishing results that identify individual children, or particular groups. Children have a right to privacy and can be very upset by being identified by name in newspapers. The media have an insatiable interest in street and working children and may make lurid use of research results. This can further stigmatise groups of children as 'criminals', 'drug addicts' or 'Aids carriers', resulting perhaps in worsening relationships with police and public.

CHILDREN'S VIEWS ON MEDIA STORIES ABOUT STREET CHILDREN

... newspapers often say a lot about the violations and terrible things and the way in which they do this is dangerous. They take the whole story and tell it all even including the name of the child and that is really ugly (Report of Honduran children to a legal enquiry on drafting a new Children's Code, 1993).

Will they talk to me?

Street children may run away from unknown adults, for a variety of reasons. Working children, likewise, have many reasons for distrusting adults or not wishing to speak to strangers. In both cases, adults may prevent the research from continuing, either unintentionally by getting in the way or speaking on the children's behalf, or intentionally because they have a vested interest in the children working. Thus the first problem in getting to speak to street and working children is one of access.

- Parents, employers and children may be unwilling for a child to take part in research because this will mean lost income. There are three ways to deal with this: making sure that research does not interfere with work; using techniques that do not take much time; replacing lost income with a payment

or by providing a service such as health care.
- Working children and the adults around them may be suspicious of researchers. Children may think you are police; parents that you are a politician or a tax inspector; employers that you are a factory inspector. These are powerful reasons not to cooperate and researchers have sometimes found themselves in physical danger, especially when crowds start taking an interest in what is going on. Police may become involved, and employers can become aggressive. Avoiding these problems is a matter of experience and, above all, sensitivity to the local context. The sudden appearance of a strange researcher, asking questions, who has not negotiated permission with research subjects is bound to raise anxieties.

PROBLEMS OF INTERVIEWING STREET CHILDREN: JOHANNESBURG

Formal interviewing was impossible for three reasons. Firstly, the children hesitated to trust information to authority figures, and formal interviewing implied authority. Secondly, their concentration spans were low due to inhaling glue fumes or to poor health. And lastly, discussion was continually interrupted by the children dashing off to guide cars into parking bays or to beg for money (Swart, 1990, p4).

A further problem, once you actually meet children in a congenial atmosphere, is finding ways of communicating with them on an equal basis. Adults almost always talk down to children, putting words into their mouths or mis-translating what they say. This has led to a tendency for adults to ask other adults (parents, teachers) about children, rather than working directly with children. Some researchers have claimed that it is impossible to work with children under five years of age. Of course it is important to talk to adults as well, but nothing substitutes for direct contact with the children themselves. And even small children have interesting, practical and decided views about their own lives. Young children should not be dismissed as informants just because their verbal skills are not the same as those of adults. In studies of homeless and working children it is inexcusable to resort to using only adult informants, given the way these children take responsibility for their own lives.

Will they tell the truth?
Western ideas about childhood include a set of contradictory notions about children's morality. On the one hand it is claimed that children are inherently

truthful, on the other that they are more likely to lie than adults. In the latter case the accusation is sometimes softened by the claim that children do not know the difference between reality and fantasy, so that although they may not be telling the truth they are not 'really' lying.

Anyone with any experience of research knows that informants often do tell lies, or at least massage the truth, for a variety of reasons. They may try to please the researcher by telling her what they think she wants to know, describe what they feel ought to happen rather than what actually happens, fob her off with any old story to get rid of her, or conceal events and facts that they are ashamed of, or which are illegal. Research may bring out any one of these responses from children, but there is no reason to suppose that they will lie more or less than adults in similar circumstances.

Lies and evasions are less likely when a researcher has built up a relationship of trust with children. This takes time and is not best achieved in the context of a one-off interview between strangers. Trust is achieved between people who know about each other. You cannot expect children to tell the truth about their lives to strangers who do not even bother to tell them about themselves, why they are asking questions, let alone ask if the questions are relevant.

TELLING LIES

Street observation showed that one of the children's main survival strategies was lie-telling in order to keep people at a distance, to generate handouts and to preserve a sympathetic view of their condition. Care had to be taken, therefore, to check the accuracy of their statements.

Telling lies is not a defence measure used only by street children. It is common in research situations ... lying enables people being investigated to control interviewers' beliefs and to influence their actions.

The street children became sufficiently well known personally during the research period for inaccurate information to be spotted and challenged. Learning how different children behaved when being evasive, and accumulating information about some of their homes from court records, helped to increase the degree of reliability in recorded information. With time, a degree of mutual trust was established which seemed to diminish the necessity for lying ... (Swart, 1990, p5).

Who should do the research?

Don't make the mistake of thinking that local people are always the best researchers. They may be middle-class professionals who find it difficult to get rapport with the children and may have to spend a lot of time getting over their own prejudices about dirty, ragged children. It is not unusual to find complaints in research reports that the children smell. Not a great deal of empathy can be achieved under such circumstances. The novelty value of a sympathetic foreigner can often elicit a good response from children, provided the researcher is not too obviously naive. However, the best field researchers are usually people from the communities themselves.

In the SABANA project that has already been mentioned the researchers were project workers who were from Smokey Mountain itself. They did not have educational qualifications, and both research and project work were learning experiences, in which they showed much creativity.

Children themselves can be excellent field investigators, as many researchers have discovered, including being involved in analysis of results. High school students have been successfully trained to do interviews and time budgets. In Zimbabwe, Pamela Reynolds used children as field assistants in her study of child work in the Zambezi Valley. She was pleased to note, after checking their accuracy, that the children 'kept detailed, careful records' (Reynolds, 1990, p55).

CHILDREN'S ATTITUDES TO BEING RESEARCHED: RURAL INDIA

They did not think it awkward that I would show some interest in what they did. The thought that I was interviewing them to write down what they said even excited them. Some became spontaneously my informants, reporting to me the news that used to go from mouth to mouth ...

I feel that most of the children I met took my questions very seriously, going, as far as they could, into the details of their work arrangements, and disclosing their conflicts, frustrations, desires and future expectations (Nieuwenhuys, 1994, pp5-6)

The importance of participation

Research with human beings is not the same as research with atoms and molecules. Human beings think, speak and have feelings. They become part of the research process. Outside researchers cannot pretend to be completely objective observers, because they too are human beings. Even if researchers only stay in a project for a few days they affect the work. The kind of answers they receive to their questions depends on the kind of people they are. Those being interviewed, for example, will have different reactions (and often give different answers) depending on whether the researcher is young or old, male or female, wealthier or poorer, local or foreign.

Thus far research has been referred to in this chapter as if it always and only included questions, in the form of interviews, questionnaires, surveys or schedules. In the eyes of the public (and, it has to be admitted, many researchers) these four terms seem to be interchangeable and to define what is expected from social research. Researchers venturing into the field without a clipboard and schedule are likely to be asked by suspicious research subjects, 'Where's your questionnaire?' In its efforts to appear as scientific as physics or chemistry, social research has come to rely heavily on the use of structured sets of questions designed to get particular information from a particular group of people – The Sample.

THE PUBLIC IMAGE OF SOCIAL RESEARCH IS THAT IT MUST BE A QUESTIONNAIRE SURVEY ...

resistance [was] mounted at the fact that I did not have a schedule of questions with a copy given in advance; my open ended questions would sometimes disturb people for they felt this was not the way to conduct research (Burra, 1987, p6).

Questionnaires and surveys have come to be the dominant model of social science. When projects think about researching the children they wish to work with, other methods are seldom considered. This is a mistake. There *is* a place in research for survey work, but this is at the end rather than the beginning of the process.

A good survey is expensive in terms of money and human resources. A bad survey gives misleading results that are likely to be based on the assumptions of the people who draw up the schedule of questions. This is potentially harmful to children and wastes resources. Unfortunately, because of the legitimacy of survey methods, few people question the method or results. In consequence, projects get locked in to repeating mistakes.

A successful survey is based on a good deal of prior research that:
- establishes the background of culture and social life;
- uses observation to develop a set of ideas (hypotheses) about the situation;
- finds out how relevant the researcher's 'problem' and hypotheses are to the people involved;
- finds out what words and ideas people use to talk about it;
- finds out about the practical social and cultural factors that affect the situation;
- develops a set of questions designed to test the hypotheses;

- tests these questions on a small group, and modifies them in the light of the responses received.

In other words, the purpose of a survey is to test results from other methods rather than to gather information in the first instance. Surveys are the final stage of the research process, they are neither the first port of call nor the only research tool.

The most appropriate way of researching social issues for project planning is action research that involves the people themselves in understanding more about their own lives and developing their own solutions to problems they have defined. The following example, adapted from the files of the YMCA of Nicaragua illustrates an effective action research project.

The community of El Cacao, Nicaragua, had lost a large proportion of its young men in the recent civil wars. Community leaders were worried that teenage girls would begin to drift to the capital, where they might end up in prostitution or on the streets. A research team was formed, consisting of the girls in the community, a theatre group and some young sociologists, all based in Managua. The girls began to research the role of young women in the community. They talked to each other, their mothers and older women about what girls should do, what they couldn't do, and what they did do. Among other things, they uncovered a level of violence against women that had previously not been discussed. The sociologists helped them to record and analyse the results. A formal academic report was written. Meanwhile, the theatre group worked with the girls on ways of communicating the results in songs and drama for the whole community. The girls discovered the problems they faced, their elders began to understand them, young men started to think about them and, together with the community leaders, they began to work on solutions that they identified for themselves. These included changing attitudes to women as might be expected, but also the less obvious solution of appropriate technology in agriculture.

Many other projects have benefited from involving participants in the research and planning process right from the start. People need to feel ownership of a project if it is to be successful, and this applies to children every bit as much as it does to adults. It is worth repeating the two basic rules for working with children everywhere:

- The main barrier is our own attitudes.
- The main resource is the children.

In the case of research, we need to throw out preconceptions about the need to use questionnaires and surveys, and the need for numerical ('quantitative') information. The first step, before you count anything, is knowing what it is you are counting. That means first gathering descriptive ('qualitative') information. It almost certainly means looking and listening before asking questions. This is not

a soft option. There are systematic methods for carrying
and even for getting quantitative results from methods oth

RESEARCH METHODS

Observation

Observation is the key to and bedrock of good research. It provides background information on the context, indicates the questions that should and should not be asked, answers a good many questions for the naive beginner, familiarises the researcher with the locality and the people in it, and raises important issues that would not have occurred to an outsider.

Observation is hard work, and probably takes up the largest proportion of research time. This is not wasted time because it shortens the time spent on other research methods and makes their results more dependable and accurate.

THE IMPORTANCE OF OBSERVATION

Street observation was a valuable means of checking the accuracy of information. A boy might say, for example, that he did not 'smoke' glue and then be seen settling down for the night with his glue bottle tucked up firmly with him (Swart, 1990, p5).

There are two types of observation, participant and structured. They are both systematic and they can be combined.

Participant observation

Participant observation means that you do not have to stand back and wait for a long time before getting involved – which is the fear of the care-filled activist, suspicious of research. It consists of essentially unstructured observations, made through being in the company of children and recorded afterwards, usually in diary form. These observations are systematic in that the focus may be on certain events or people, or at certain places or particular times. Usually the diary record begins by recording everything that occurs and then gradually begins to concentrate on particular regularities or unusual occurrences. You will find it essential to make notes regularly, and as soon as possible after a period of observation, otherwise you are likely to forget many of the rich details of your experiences.

Many academic researchers have argued that it is impossible to do participant vation with children because the researcher cannot participate as a child. But this argument could apply to participant observation with any group Participation simply means taking part in social life in some way that is appropriate for the researcher and the people being researched. Among adults a woman cannot participate as a man, or a young man as a grandfather. But researchers have found many acceptable roles by which they can participate and from which they can observe. Often this is by exploiting a skill they have, such as being able to fill in forms for people with limited literacy; or the abilities they do not have, so that they become pupils in language or in learning new crafts.

Experiences of participant observation with street and working children have shown three approaches to be useful:

- **Go where the children are**

  Participant observation means going to where the children are, watching, recording and reacting. SABANA started its observations at the very top of the dump known as Smokey Mountain where there was an unused, derelict building on which the researchers obtained a temporary lease (Gunn & Ostos, 1992).

  Street children are not so easy to observe because of their nomadic habits. You need to map the territory, finding out where they hang out at different times of day and, rather than following them around (which is tiring and intrusive), make staggered observations at fixed locations.

- **Provide a service**

  This is an option for participant observation that has been taken by many researchers. It is a first step in action research and puts the stress on participation. SABANA noticed that children had to buy water by the glass in the dust, and that this meant they drank less than they needed working in the heat and dust. So the project arranged for barrels of water daily. The children could drink and even wash their hands. Slowly they began to drift in and get to know the staff:

  'It emerged that their first priority was a place to rest out of the sun and a flat place where they could play. With the assistance of a few mothers, project workers responded to this request by clearing the area around the building and enclosing it with a fence made out of discarded bedsprings. Lured by balls and simple games, the children began to flock in' (Gunn & Ostos, 1992, p633).

  Primary health care can be a very important service for street children, but this should be out on the streets, not in a purpose-built centre. Services should be provided, as Mark Connolly says with 'no questions asked and no values imposed' (Connolly, 1990b, p135).

- **Observe the wider context**
  It is important to learn about the place of work in children's lives as a whole. Olga Nieuwenhuys found this in her study of working children in Kerala:

  'We did not limit ourselves to observing the work floor but soon were found at all hours of the day observing children: in front of shops, near market places, near ponds and wells, along tracks, on grazing grounds, on the beach, in kitchens, classrooms, Koranic schools, the nursery school etc. In this way we were able to map a wide range of activities carried out by children without having to decide a priori whether they could be called "work" or not' (Nieuwenhuys, 1994, p33).

OBSERVING BY BEING WITH STREET CHILDREN: THE *GAMINES* OF BOGOTÁ

In urban areas where groups of *gamines* were concentrated, there was rarely a moment when I was not interacting with children. The basic health care services were provided informally, because *gamines* are very active and mobile during the daytime. A lot of time was spent conversing with street boys, listening to their stories, and just watching the 'street action'. This interaction with the *gamines* frequently attracted attention, and passers-by would often stop to warn me that my young companions were dangerous and not to be trusted. Also, on a few occasions the police were suspicious of these activities, resulting in my being searched and questioned (Connolly, 1990b, p135).

Structured observation

There are a number of ways in which observations can be structured to answer questions or test hypotheses that have arisen from participant observation. You may want to know how much time a child spends in a particular task each day, for example. Or you may be wondering what street children get up to when they are in a particular part of town: Whom do they talk to? Do they play? Work? Fight? And how long do they spend doing each of these?

Structured observations usually require concentrated effort, using prepared schedules in which the observer records a number of categorised activities, as they occur, for frequency and duration. They are made at specified intervals which could be:

- once a day, at the same time (this captures regularity at a peak time of day,

    such as traffic rush hours for children who sell to motorists);
- at different times of day throughout a week or a longer period of time (to examine daily routines);
- at four, five, six or eight-day intervals (in order to check weekly routines);
- spot checks or routine observations over longer periods of time (to look at seasonal changes).

Observations can be made of single children or groups of children. In rural situations, or in workshops and factories, it may be particularly interesting to look at the activities of individual children over time, comparing what is done by children of different ages, or the tasks performed by boys and girls. This is easiest when you can be more or less sure where a particular child may be found at any time. With street children, on the other hand, group dynamics may be more important to know about. Which children gather at the railway station around eight o'clock at night, what do they do, how do they behave?

    It can be helpful to use two researchers simultaneously to cross check, or one to observe and one to record. If the circumstances permit, you can also cross check with the children under observation to see if you have made a correct interpretation of their behaviour.

    An observation schedule need not be complex. First you have to decide from unstructured observation what things you want to examine further. Then draw up a simple chart that can be easily reproduced. If you make it too complex it will be time-consuming to analyse. You will probably have to test it out a few times before you get it right. Some examples to set you thinking are given in Appendix 2.

    After spending more than a year studying child labour in the Zambezi valley by a variety of methods, Pamela Reynolds reports that systematic observation at five-minute intervals over a one or two-hour period:

> provided the most reliable and comprehensive records of children's work. It was the only way to capture context. Relationships between those who gave orders or requests for tasks to be performed and those who received and carried out the work could be noted. Ruses for avoiding work, generosity in assuming another's task, and the manner in which children cared for the elderly and the young were observed. The technique allowed for the recording of multiple task performance: one girl, for example, was in charge of a toddler while she prepared relish for the evening meal and watched over water heating for her father's bath (Reynolds, 1990, p76).

But she adds that this method is time-consuming and involves too few research subjects. It is also an imposition on the lives of others, relying on trust, which is not easily won.

Spot observations, regular observations of a child over the research period, allow standardised information to be gathered with less disruption, and can also be used to get recall data (see page 69).

It must be remembered that time-use surveys do not measure energy and effort, which are really important for children who may be working at tasks more suited to older, bigger people, and with tools that are too large for them. This could be a crucial factor for looking at the bad effects of working on children.

More participatory methods

Focus group discussion

Focus group discussions have become popular within project work for dealing with difficult topics, particularly with adolescents and often related to work on sexuality and HIV infection. However, they are also a useful research tool. They can take place at any time during the research process and are especially useful in the early stages for discovering what different groups of local people think about topics such as childhood, work and street children and the language they use to talk about them.

A focus group discussion, when used for research purposes, is rather like a conversational interview, but with a group of about 6 to 12 individuals, who are usually all the same type of people – in other words, all street children, or all project workers. The conversation is 'focused' in the sense that it concentrates on a single theme or issue, such as 'children' or 'work'. The advantage of focus group discussions is that they can give an idea about what the general opinion is among a wide group of people at any time. They are not, in general, useful for quantitative work.

Focus group discussions can work quite well with children, who are often more talkative in a group than alone with an adult – the strength of numbers evens out the power relationship somewhat. They have been found to be useful for finding out about sensitive issues, about sex for example, particularly when they take place on a regular basis with the same group, which can build a sense of solidarity and trust.

Children with less structured lives may find it difficult to cope with structured focus group discussions, as a Childhope research team found in Nairobi. This group of children from a street children project was taken out of town for a residential period to talk about HIV infection and Aids. The researchers noted that these young people needed to be motivated to continue with discussions by means of 'songs and games to maintain concentration' (Barker & Mbogori, 1992, p7).

Nevertheless, in a less formal environment in South Africa, Jill Swart was able to hold 50 discussions with a total of 178 children, most of whom took part in more than one. She did not propose themes to the children, and allowed them the freedom of her house, including the swimming pool, with children choosing the topics they wanted to discuss and focusing on these guided by researchers (Swart, 1990, p3). The conversation would simply begin with an overview of the day, and a topic would be drawn from it. The success of this, compared to the Childhope experience, was due to the fact that it was child-centred – concentrating on topics that were of interest to the children at that time. Just because adults are worried about the spread of HIV among street children does not mean that this is seen as a 'problem' by the children themselves.

The basic requirements for successful focus group discussions are:
- a comfortable place, where there will be no interruptions;
- an informal atmosphere;
- equality and trust between the discussants and facilitators;
- understanding and agreement within the group about the purpose of the discussion;
- respect for all participants – everyone has a right to speak and be listened to, no one is allowed to dominate the group;
- an agreed and open method of recording – flip charts, tape recorders and videos have been used; flip charts are more open, they can be displayed around the room for participants to check what has gone before, and participants can take part in and agree to the content of a flip chart record; in addition, sound tape and video recordings are expensive and time-consuming to analyse.

Drawings

Drawings of various aspects of life can be extremely helpful research tools when working with respondents who are shy, illiterate, inarticulate or simply of another group with different conceptual structures. Drawings can break down barriers. You don't have to use words and they are usually fun to do. The main points to remember are that children of different ages draw in quite distinct ways, and that the way things are seen and drawn varies between cultures. Thus you need to be careful about interpretation, and to cross check with children as well as with people from the same cultural group.

INTERPRETING DRAWINGS

The importance of supplementary explanation is clear when we consider that Sipho (14) and Meshak (15) both had an obsession with drawing graves, but that they drew them for different reasons.

Sipho's preoccupation derived from having lost both his parents; his mother died first, then his father. He had been estranged from his brothers and sisters by a fight at his mother's graveside and graves seemed to have become a symbol of his unhappiness.

In contrast, when Meshak was asked why he drew graves so compulsively, even on his school books, he replied, 'Graves is good. I think of my Granny. She loved me.' Alongside one of the graves he drew a table set with candles and flowers. He used to do this for his grandmother. For Meshak, unlike Sipho, the grave symbolises joy and peace and he appears to draw strength and inspiration from its image (Swart, 1990, p26).

Jill Swart and Chris Williams developed drawings as research tools in their work with street children in Johannesburg looking at children's moral values (Swart, 1988 and 1990). They collected three sets of drawings:

- Spontaneous – which added information to what the children said verbally; children 'often asked for notepaper and a pen or pencil with which to illustrate their verbal communications. They were also encouraged to illustrate situations which they found difficult to describe verbally'.
- Informal thematic – 'provided new insights into previously unexplored areas of the children's lives as well as validating statements made previously by them' (Swart, 1990, p13). Themes might be 'home life' ('Me at Home'), 'running away' 'smoking glue'.
- Formal thematic – sessions in which a fixed number of children drew 'good' and 'bad' things and 'a bad person'. These drawings could be used for producing quantitative information. Swart and Williams collected 69 drawings from a total of 36 children. The ideas of badness and goodness were reflected in the number of drawings on each topic.

Good Characteristic	No. of Drawings	Bad Characteristic	No. of Drawings
Service to others	11	Physical violence	32
Kindness to others	11	Theft	27
Church attendance and prayer	11	Killing	20
Helpfulness	8	Glue sniffing	12
Kindness to animals	6	Not conforming	12
Loving others	6	Cruelty to children	8
Conforming	6	Dangerous driving	5
Obedience	3	Cruelty to animals	4
Courage	2	Criminal activities	2
Sharing	1	Disrespect	2
		Arson	1

Table of good and bad characteristics derived from street children's drawings in South Africa (adapted from Swart, 1990)

The potential of drawings for producing quantitative as well as qualitative information has been shown by a number of researchers who use drawings to carry out 'surveys without questionnaires'. One example, again from the SABANA project on Smokey Mountain, illustrates the advantage of using researchers from the local community who are also project workers. They arrived at a creative solution to the problem of carrying out a household survey in a particularly suspicious group:

> Smokey Mountain residents were notoriously adept at delivering 'misinformation', particularly about family finances, so the Community Workers developed a unique and extremely effective mode of conducting their interviews. The 'questionnaire' consisted of a blank sheet on which the interviewer would sketch an outline of the household being interviewed, showing rooms and precise type of appliances (to denote economic status) and the residents and their relationship to each other. Only the picture was recorded at the time of the interview in consideration of the sensitivities of the respondents, but immediately afterwards the interviewer would record the questions asked and answers received and place the information in the child's envelope (Gunn & Ostos, 1992, p637).

Some researchers have used drawings in the course of individual case studies, or to examine self-esteem, intelligence and neurological functioning among groups of street and working children. There are several, well-tested psychological tests for doing this. They can be useful but they are best administered and interpreted by psychologists (see Aptekar, 1988).

Other methods in which children can participate

Recall methods

As Pamela Reynolds points out, finding out how children's time is spent using structured observation methods is time-consuming, and covers only a small number of children (Reynolds, 1990). A faster, although less accurate method, in which a number of children can take part, is to ask people to recall what has happened in the recent past. The recall period may be the previous 24 hours, week or fortnight. Longer periods are not recommended, especially for children. Recall has been used to find out about:

- the tasks and activities of children;
- children's diets;
- illnesses and accidents.

Time recall charts are similar to the structured observation charts shown earlier. If children are literate they can fill in their own charts, or you can use school children as assistants. Make sure you are using the same words and that the children understand them. It is always worthwhile checking this, even when it seems obvious what words mean. Researchers asking street children about episodes of diarrhoea in Calcutta found that some children thought this meant passing too much urine!

An example of this kind of method is the 'Chore Chart' used to find out about the relationship between school work, domestic tasks and paid work among children in Lagos state, Nigeria.

> After a preliminary intensive chore observation of some children, a chore chart was drawn up representing every day of the week and three periods of the day. For a chosen school week, each child was interviewed three times a day – to minimise under-reporting due to faulty recall ... the children were not confronted with a prepared list of chores, rather they were presented with a time period and requested to recall carefully all the actions, chores and non-chores in which they had participated within the specified period. Children were then asked appropriate structured questions about the tasks (Beatrice Adenike Oloko, 1990, p4).

Information from school children

It is a mistake to think that children are divided into two groups – those who go to school and those who work. Many children work in order to be able to afford school uniforms and books and a good way to obtain information about working children is by cooperating with schools. This is especially important for looking at the effects of work on schooling (and vice versa), or at the 'at-risk' children who may be on the point of dropping out of school. In addition, school children have been found to be good research assistants.

School-based research is useful for:
- finding points of intervention for prevention and development;
- getting large quantities of information about children who combine work and school.

The disadvantages are:
- it is not so useful if you want to provide services for drop outs;
- you may obtain so much information that it will cause problems for analysis;
- the children are in an authority situation, they may write to please the teacher rather than telling the truth (although the evidence is that this is not a major problem).

COMBINING SCHOOL AND WORK IN PERU

Every day I go to work with my father in Lima. I work in a wholesale business. In order to go to work I get up every day at two in the morning. And I have to get up early because in Lima I have to start work at 4.30. I work till 11 in the morning. Then I come home and have lunch with my mother and then I go to school. I don't even have time to help my mother (essay on 'What I do when I am not in school' by a 13-year-old boy, collected by Judith Ennew and William Paredes in 1982).

Methods to find out children's feelings and opinions

One of the problems with all projects, but particularly those providing services, is that it is not always possible to know if what is being provided is what people want and need. This can be a particular problem in work with street and working children:
- because they may find it difficult to express their feelings in ways we understand;
- because we do not listen to what they say when they do express their feelings;
- because they are developing emotional skills rapidly and we assume that they are being hopelessly damaged by their experiences;

• because we think we know how they feel and what they want and need.

All these difficulties are the result of thinking that children are not competent and cannot cope with difficult situations from which they need to be rescued by adults. Some children clearly are damaged in mind and body by the work they do and the lives they lead. But, absolute crisis situations apart, it is wiser to start planning projects on the basis of what they _can_ do and _can_ cope with. Discovering this need not mean using complex psychological tests: much will be learned from focus group discussions. For more detailed work on coping patterns and self-image you may have to be innovative or to call on the expertise of academic researchers.

For example, one study of Smokey Mountain children used a questionnaire that elicited responses to 'hypothetical but typical crisis situations'. The object was to look at children's coping mechanisms (which turned out to be good). The answers were scored 'depending on the degree of immediacy, self-reliance and effort indicated using a six-point scale' (Pangan, 1992, p3). These questionnaires, incidentally, were administered by high school pupils.

Another group of authors reports a comparison between street youth in Bogotá and Washington DC. They asked open-ended questions about life and experiences and also asked the young people to rate themselves on a five-point scale 'to measure psychosocial competence and environmental variables … [they] rated their perceptions of their own self-efficacy, trust and levels of coping in four settings: in general, at home, in institutions, and on the street. They also rated the personal and physical supports and threats in those settings'. The rank scale was the sum of ratings in each category (Tyler et al, 1992). This research was carried out in the context of long-term relationships with children in projects after the method had been taught to project workers in intensive training. The academic researchers had been asked by the project to design the research method and the whole process was the result of close collaboration.

Also in Bogotá, a YMCA project involved in long-term work with street children's families used counselling-based techniques that combined project work and data gathering. Family histories were gathered using drawings of family trees, and family functioning explored using discussion of the importance of the family, how the family reacts to difficult situations (such as death, illness, debt, cash shortage) and to 'nice' things (defined as 'nice' by the families rather than the project worker). Other psychological techniques included sentence completion games, story games and making and discussing collages. This research is also the result of collaboration between academics and project workers.

STUDYING CHILDREN

Children's worlds are not easy to record. To do so, we need to draw on the methods already elaborated in anthropology, sociology, psychology ... but we need to innovate beyond these in devising techniques to capture and account for children's behaviour, attitudes, motives and contexts (Reynolds, 1990, p161).

Checking and recording

By this stage you should have:
- a good collection of background material on children in general and street and/or working children in particular;
- information from observation and other methods, such as drawings, about the group of children you would like to work with;
- information from focus group discussions about what the local community, including the children, thinks about general issues, such as childhood and work, and the specific problems of the group of children you would like to work with.

You will need to check these different pieces of information against each other, for there may well be contradictions or further questions raised. At this point it may be appropriate to use a survey questionnaire. It is on the basis of this material that you will:
- select the target group and objectives for your project;
- start to think about the methods and techniques you will use for working;
- decide on the criteria you will use for measuring progress.

As these are fundamental issues it is worth taking further time to discus them with the people you expect to benefit from the project, if this is at all possible. There certainly should be consultation with local groups that might be affected by the project as well as with actual or potential project workers. This means setting aside sufficient time, at least in blocks of whole days, when groups can meet without interruption and use focus group discussion methods. If at all possible, use a facilitator to make sure the job gets done.

Censuses, surveys, questionnaires and interview schedules

There are many confusions in the use of terms such as census, survey, questionnaire and interview. It helps to think of them all as ways of viewing a group of people:

- A census is a numerical account of how many there are in the group and aspects of some of their basic characteristics.
- A questionnaire is a method of finding out more about them, using a structured set of questions, which can be administered impersonally (by post, for example) as well as face-to-face.
- An interview is another method of finding out more, in a structured conversation between the researcher and a number of people in the group, either using a schedule like a questionnaire or simply covering a number of topics decided in advance by the researcher.
- A survey can be any of the above.

All have been used with street and working children.

Counting children

Much of the difficulty in carrying out a census of street and/or working children is caused by differences of opinion about definitions. However, it is often necessary to have some idea of how many children are at risk, whether they are 'on' or 'of' the street, or less visible working children. Funding bodies, the media and government agents all tend to ask the question 'How many?'.

- In the case of street children it is difficult to make an accurate count because of their mobility.
- In the case of working children it is difficult to come up with an accurate number because they are largely hidden.

The pressure to count street children is usually more acute and you can guarantee that whatever number you come up with will be challenged. Government agents are likely to say you are exaggerating, the public and the media will accuse you of playing down the problem. Given that anyone with an interest in street children will probably draw the line differently between street and working children you will find the census issue one of the most frustrating exercises in the whole project.

The first thing to do is to use the research process you have followed so far to come up with a working definition of your target population or populations (for example, you may decide to work providing services to children in crisis situations at the same time as preventative work with 'at-risk' children in the community).

Then you need to find some reasonably accurate way to count the total number of children in each category. That will give you some idea of the scale of the problem and also allow you to plan which children within the total group you will target for your project.

Methods that have been used to count street children are:

- Something akin to the capture/release methods of animal behaviourists; children have their hands stamped when they are counted by teams of researchers so that they are not counted more than once on the same night; this may be efficient – but is it ethical?
- Day and night-time counts at known gathering places (as many as three times in 24 hours); researchers need to be familiar with certain children so that they are not counted twice; teams of researchers can cover larger metropolitan areas by going out to count simultaneously; ideally this should be done on different days of the week and at different times of the year to capture seasonal changes.

Ultimately, whatever method is used will depend on the local circumstances and not be absolutely accurate. Such an approximation is no problem provided that the definitions of groups of children counted, the methods used and the possible sources of inaccuracy are made clear in any reports. Much time and energy have been wasted on bitter arguments about the number of children on the street or working in certain cities according to the various 'counts' of NGOs, police and government. These efforts would have been better directed at helping children.

COUNTING STREET CHILDREN IN ASUNCIÓN

In taking a census of working street children one encounters various difficulties; the number varies according to the hour of the day and to the work they do because of the schedules required by the different occupations. They are constantly on the move, changing types of work, and sometimes doing several jobs at the same time. The season and the climate also influence this type of census …

Our procedure favoured children with the following characteristics: between 7 and 15 years of age, not too shy, rather open towards strangers, performing jobs that allow for longer conversations while they are working, and working at places that were not too heavily controlled by third parties who could interfere (*Working in the streets*, pp17 and 14).

Issues of sampling

Because of the difficulty of counting street and working children, selecting a proper 'scientific' sample by random methods is impossible. Unless you know how many there are in the first place you simply cannot do this. The best method is what is called 'opportunistic sampling', which basically means the best group you can manage! Once again, if methods and research problems are made clear in any reports the research results are valid. Thus it is perfectly acceptable to note, as researchers did in Indore, India, that:

> Since the street children keep on moving it would have been very difficult to prepare any sampling frame, out of which to select the desired sample applying principles of random method. Instead, the places where the children were generally found were selected. The trained investigators visited these places three times a day.
>
> The places visited by the investigators for locating the street children were the railway platform, bus stands, parking places in the main market, footpaths, tea stalls, hotels, garages, etc.
>
> There is no way by which the representative nature of the sample can be verified except to say that the children have been selected from a very wide variety of job situations, which may ensure a good representation (Phillips, 1992, p23).

Unfortunately, even experienced researchers do not always follow this procedure. Thus it is possible to read in the literature on street children that '10% of street children are girls', or '25% of street children in Colombia come from mother-headed households', without any reference to the size of sample these findings were based on, or the cities in which the studies took place. It is in this way that mythical 'facts' enter the public image of street and working children.

Surveys

As we have already seen, surveys rightly belong at the end of the research process and may not always need a questionnaire. Prior research establishes how relevant the 'problem' seen by outsiders is to the people being researched, the social and cultural background and – very important this – the language in which people discuss them.

The framing of questions used in survey questionnaires is a very skilled job and needs a good deal of testing to get it right. In a survey of street children in Bombay it was found that the ideas of time span used in the questions were unfamiliar to the children. This has many causes. If you don't have a watch and you don't have appointments to keep, why is the time of day relevant? Children asked 'How long have you been on the street?' did not know if this referred to the amount of time that day or in their entire lifetime. Questions concerning a child's age also raised complications. If you don't go to school, or have a birth certificate, why is your age relevant? A child's approximate age can be judged by using 'time-line' techniques, which entail finding out about important events in the area over the last twenty years or more (such as earthquake, general strikes and so forth) and then asking parents if the child was born in the same year. But this complicates questionnaire design. And the question has to be phrased carefully. It is all too easy to ask a mother when a particular child was born and receive an answer such as 'In the summer time'. The Bombay researchers also found that they needed different questions for children who lived with their families and children who did not. They found themselves increasingly frustrated with the carefully constructed questionnaire from a research institute and made 'separate notings … of interesting facts concerning the lives of the children even if the interview schedule did not contain such references' (D'Lima & Gosalia, 1992, p101).

This may well be the time to rely on the skills of an outside researcher but, to check on the product, and also in order to be able to read reports from other research, it is worth having some idea about survey techniques. Some references to basic textbooks are listed in Appendix 3. However, it is worth noting the following factors:

- Surveys, interviews and questionnaires use schedules of questions that are either 'closed' or 'open-ended'. Closed questions provide a series of possible responses (Yes, No, Don't Know, for example) that are pre-coded for computer analysis. The advantage is that they are quick to administer and analyse. The disadvantage is that the person being interviewed has few options for response, all of which reflect the ideas of the person who designed the schedule. Open-ended questions allow the person being interviewed to express themselves more freely – for example in response to a question such as 'What do you think of street children?'. The disadvantage is that replies may be long and difficult and time-consuming to analyse. Many researchers make their reports as if open-ended questions make research participatory. This is not the case unless based on prior participatory techniques and drawn up by participants, which could equally well apply to a schedule of closed questions.

- Both open-ended and closed questionnaires require skilled and trained interviewers and analysts. Many researchers make the mistake of using schedules developed elsewhere. This is never acceptable. Be critical of survey results that already exist – get hold of a copy of the list of questions or 'schedule' (which is often printed at the back of the report), and ask yourself if these were good questions in that context. Then read the report with this in mind. A survey is not good just because it uses fancy techniques such as multiple regression analysis. Bad surveys can usually be judged by the number of case studies used in the report and the fact that these bear little relationship to the reported survey results.

Interviewing techniques

PROBLEMS OF INTERVIEWING STREET CHILDREN: BOMBAY

Milling crowds of people move in and out of the stations fanning out in all directions on the road. Street children are found precisely in the vicinity of such railway stations, street junctions, bridges and half-dug pavements. The atmosphere for interviewing was constantly charged with movement and noise which made concentration difficult. Such interviews also arouse the curiosity of passers-by as well as other street children and, if not the interviewer, the interviewee often gets distracted. Some children were cooperative and happy to talk to a caring adult; for others it was a repeat performance, the outcome of which they were not too sure; for still others it was a way of having fun at the investigator's expense. The investigators developed the capacity to conduct interviews in the most varied settings: in playgrounds and on footpaths; on parapets, platforms near railway tracks, and the like. It had to be a friendly chat. Paper jottings had to be made not during interviews, but later somewhere in the noise and bustle of the area before the facts became too mixed up to sort out. Most of the interviews took place in the late hours of the evening (D'Lima & Gosalia, 1992, pp10-11).

Interviews are often confused with questionnaires. They can be very structured or simply an account of a recalled conversation. They are best described as structured conversations. They can be carried out with individuals or groups (in which case they may be focus group discussions). An interview gives a lot more space to what the interviewee wants to say than is possible with a fixed questionnaire schedule.

Interviews can be used with street and working children, provided that they are carried out in the context of ongoing relationships with them. They are not successful if the interviewer is a stranger – much information *is* gathered in this way, but it is of doubtful value. For some reason, many researchers choose to call one-off interviews, that are really questionnaires using open-ended questions or schedules asking personal questions about themes such as sexual activity, 'in-depth' interviews. This is incorrect. In-depth interviews take place over time, at different times with the same individuals, in the context of an ongoing relationship with the researcher. They are usually combined with other methods that cross-check the information gathered.

Jill Swart's work with street children in Johannesburg illustrates the use of interviews in an in-depth process. She used interviews of up to an hour and a half to gather case study material from 15 children to supplement information gathered by other means. 'Because of their nomadism it was impossible to use formal sampling procedures', so she selected children who seemed to her to represent a cross-section of street children and asked them if they would like to talk about their lives in order to help other children by helping people learn about their realities. An average of eight interviews was carried out with each child (Swart, 1990, p4).

All interviews require a situation in which both the researcher and the child are relaxed and the child does not feel intimidated. The main requirements are:

- a quiet place, with just the two of you, free from interruptions and distractions;
- removal of all possible reminders of adult power – you should not sit behind a desk or on a higher place, for example;
- an agreed time frame – with street and working children it is more sensible to refer to a regular event, such as the arrival of a particular bus, than a measured period of time, such as an hour;
- plenty of warm-up discussion, in which the interviewer talks about his or her own life and the reasons for the research as well as familiarising the child with the method of recording the interview;
- as few questions as possible and the minimum of interruptions once a child has begun to talk; don't interpose your own ideas and experiences; don't make judgements on what the child is saying; and if he or she begins (in your opinion) to stray off the subject keep listening – you might hear something much more interesting than you had expected;
- keep your first questions open-ended and general; it is better to begin by asking less personal questions, such as 'I'm interested in shoeshiners, are there many around here?' (even if you know the answer – or think you do), than to go straight into a battery of detailed enquiries about the child's age, family life, length of time as a shoeshiner, earnings and so forth; you can ask supplementary questions later, to fill in the details of the overall picture given by the child;
- show your interest and be encouraging, by giving the child your full attention, smiling, nodding your head or in whatever way is appropriate in the local culture.

ONGOING RESEARCH AND MONITORING

The information you will have already gathered on the target group of children serves as the baseline data for the project. You need to know more about these children, as individuals and as a group, as time goes on, in order to check their progress and to see if the project's objectives are being fulfilled (indeed, you will also need to check from time to time if the objectives are still appropriate).

To do this you will need some methods of recording information on a day-to-day basis. Some projects devise registration forms, but these can be time-consuming to fill in and may daunt project workers who are tired, busy and don't like writing anyway. In any case, because each child is an individual he or she may not fit comfortably on the form! There are other, simpler options. In the SABANA project, record-keeping was combined with ongoing research. Dossiers on individual children were kept in the context of project development. Research and record-keeping were carried out by community workers from the area, for whom the research was simultaneously a capacity-building activity.

> When a child came to the Center for the first time, a large envelope bearing his or her name was prepared and placed in a file. At each subsequent visit, the [Community Workers] would make a note about the service provided and any new information learned about the child and place it in the envelope. These envelopes constituted a constantly expanding dossier on each child and, although dusty and dishevelled, they were highly practical given the conditions at the Drop In Center and the still rudimentary bookkeeping skills of the [Community Workers]. The data they provided were useful for various purposes: for example, an accurate count of the child scavengers, the database for subsequent studies, and anecdotal material to guide the counselling of individual children (Gunn & Ostos, 1992, p637).

As the project develops you will also need to develop a set of monitoring indicators, in order to check the progress of the project. These can be based on statistical information or descriptive data. It all depends what the project workers think should be monitored at that stage of the project's life. Some information, such as how many children participate in the project on a regular basis, is numerical and collecting it is probably part of day-to-day activities. At other times it may be important to check on the effects of changes in the local situation – if there are changes in police activities or an increase in adult unemployment for example. Or you might want to assess the effects of innovations in the project itself. The table of indicators drawn up by SCF's programme for street children in Jamaica in 1994, after nearly eight years' work, shows how a variety of aspects can be monitored by different methods at any one time.

THE SCF JAMAICA INDICATORS

Target area	Indicator	Method
CHILDREN (1) Children in urgent or crisis situations	(1) Violence: trend in group	(1) Against children: headcount (2) In the children: drawings, focus group discussions, role play
	(2) Infectious diseases: trend in group	Head count (NB: needs control group)
(2) Children whose need is not so immediate	(1) Level of involvement in work, individual and group trends	(1) Working activities (2) Time spent hustling each day
	(2) Parental contact	Head count (noting gender and age differences)
PARENTS	(1) Attitudes of parents of marginalised youth	Attitude/knowledge change
	(2) Take up of programme for parents	Head count
	(3) Spin off	Activity audit
	(4) Networking	Existence of parent group Activities of group over time Involvement in project
COMMUNITY	(1) How much does the community know about the project?	FGD,* opinion leaders and institutions
	(2) Perceptions of the project	FGD, inhabitants (especially children)
SOCIETY	(1) Influencing policy on children's rights	List activities Evaluate
	(2) Influencing policy on parenting – influencing policy – promoting programmes – development and dissemination of materials – involvement in networks	Interviews opinion leaders and institution workers

* FGD = focus group discussion

Programme indicators can cover a range of topics that concern the children, the staff, the project and its relationships with the outside world. Much will depend on the services provided, or the development methods used to work with the children, which will be discussed in the next chapter. The following list should start you thinking about themes that could be chosen to monitor project progress:

For the children:

Improved social skills
- fewer fights
- more sharing
- more caring behaviour
- better physical appearance
- fewer illnesses or injuries

Improved life chances
- improved literacy and numeracy
- entries to formal school system
- acquisition of skills for the job market
- finding a job, being adequately self-employed

For the project:
- attendance records
- events/excursions
- meals, health checks and other services
- staff training/development
- links with other organisations/institutions
- involvement in advocacy and policy

QUESTIONS TO ASK YOURSELF

You should now be able to think about what methods might be suitable given your time and resources, the children you would like to work with and the local situation. The research experiences of other projects can be used to start designing your process of gathering baseline data to start a project and ongoing investigations to measure its progress. For technical details of research methods you should consult one of the other books given in the reference chapter on research methods at the end of the manual (see p176). SCF is also publishing a volume on *Assessment, monitoring, review and evaluation* in the development manual series.

The basic questions you need to keep in mind are:
- What are local attitudes towards and ideas about childhood, child workers

and street children?
- How will children and other project participants be involved in the research process?
- In view of your survey of secondary sources, discussions with local people and potential project participants, what do you really need to know in order to start the project?
- Do children and other project participants agree that these are the things you really need to know?
- What local research expertise can you count on?
- If you are working with outside researchers, have you drawn up and agreed terms of reference with them?
- What are the most appropriate methods of research:
  - for the children?
  - for you?
  - for the project?
  - ethically?
- If you are thinking of using a survey or questionnaire:
  - has it been drawn up on the basis of prior, in-depth, local research?
  - were the children involved in developing it?
  - do the questions use words and ideas that the children understand?
  - are the questions really relevant?
  - do you have trained interviewers?
  - has the schedule been piloted?
  - do you have the resources to make a proper analysis of the answers?
- How are you going to use the results of research?

Chapter 5

PROJECT OPTIONS

There is a single rule to use as a guide in project work:
- The emphasis should not be on making children leave the streets or stop work, but on increasing the range of choices available to them and helping them to make their own decisions.

Unfortunately there are barriers you will encounter in project work, from the public and often from those who wish to fund projects to help street children:
- the desire to rescue the children;
- the urge to find a quick, neat solution;
- the tendency towards welfare handouts rather than a durable solution.

WHAT THE PUBLIC WANTS FROM PROJECTS

Accustomed to being the target of contempt, scavenger children would freeze into silence or scatter at the approach of strangers. No one knew how many there were, how they felt, or what they really needed. Although easy to see, they were hard to reach. At the same time, there was great pressure to act quickly. The project was funded for only two years, an impossibly short time to develop, implement and institutionalise such work; and many in the Philippines, appalled and embarrassed by the pathetic appearance of these children, demanded drastic solutions such as bulldozing the dump, or relocating all the children in youth centres (Gunn & Ostos, 1992, p632).

THE FRAMEWORK OF PROJECTS

Project planning consists of:
- finding out where you are (through the information-gathering and research process discussed in the last two chapters);
- deciding where you want to be (defining objectives);
- choosing ways of achieving those objectives.

The overall objective of all projects with street and working children is to help them improve their lives. This is obvious, but is not as simple as it sounds. You

need to decide, *with them*, exactly what improvements are needed and possible. This means asking the following questions:
- Which children have the most urgent needs and problems?
- How do they define these?
- How can these needs be met or problems answered in the best possible way?
- What are other local projects and programmes doing?
- Where are the gaps in provision?
- What skills and resources can your project count on?

These questions will help you decide on both objectives and target groups. Many of the answers will already have been provided by the research process. However, in answering these questions two important considerations should be borne in mind:
- **A balance should be struck** between providing services, which is only a short-term solution, and bringing about long-term improvements in these children's lives.
- **All non-governmental work is limited in scope**. The real solutions to the problems lie in the hands of governments, both nationally and in international relations.

To be truly effective in achieving its objectives the project must develop work at four levels. Both the objectives (policies) and target groups (people) should be deliberately focused on:
- children;
- parents and families;
- local communities;
- national and international campaigning and advocacy.

TARGET GROUPS – PEOPLE ISSUES

Children

Fabio Dallape makes a distinction, from his experience with the Undugu Society, between three different groups of children, which is potentially more useful for project planning than the disputed distinction between children 'in' and 'of' the streets and can also apply to working children:
- children who come from rural areas and would be willing to go back;
- children who live in gangs in towns, and have contact with their families;
- children who are completely on their own.

Two further categories of working children should be added:
- children in rural or urban areas who live permanently with their families and go out to work, in the streets, in factories and workshops, in agriculture;
- child domestic workers and others who live with employers, in workshops and, for some child prostitutes, in brothels.

Some projects emphasise the particular vulnerability of street girls and treat them differently. But you must have good reasons for making distinctions. For example, one project of Child Workers in Nepal made a particular priority of rescuing girls and placing them in residential accommodation because of what the project saw as the special dangers they ran on the streets. The girls ran back to the streets. The project had made the mistake of thinking that the girls' 'special vulnerability' gave them a right to be more protective. But girls have a right to participate in decisions made about them, and can be every bit as independently minded as boys. They are people too, not just objects of concern; this applies to all especially vulnerable groups. In any case, the particular danger to which girls are exposed is presumably sexual exploitation. Emphasis on this shows two kinds of prejudices. On the one hand it sees girls only in their sexual role. On the other, it ignores the sexual exploitation of boys on the streets.

When you are selecting a target group of children from the situations you have researched, it is worth remembering the litany of hazards: too young, too hard, too long, and so forth, from page 29. This will help you to decide on priority groups.

It is also important to be aware of the provision made by other projects. Some groups, such as street children, can be very fashionable. Others, such as child domestic workers, receive scarcely any project attention. Try not to be the seventh project for ragpickers in the same location in a single town (it does happen!).

Parents, families and communities

In most cases the target groups of parents, families and communities will follow from the target group of children. However, there are some factors to remember:
- Do not target mother-headed families or step-families for special attention unless this is indicated by research that has compared children in the target group with other children with the same economic background who are not street or working children.
- Remember that 'family' means different things in different cultures; do not impose Western values and do not assume that family support only comes from parents – grandparents, brothers and sisters, cousins, aunts and uncles all have roles to play.

- Remember that children may come from one community and live or work in another. Which community is the most relevant for the child, which can give the most support?
- Also remember that communities are complex groups of individuals; contacting parents is not the same as community work and there may be different (and opposing) community leaders; it is all too easy to end up working with only one section of the community.

Local development and children's needs

There are two possible community development options:
- Working with the community in which the children live now.
- Working with the community where the children come from.

Most development work relevant to street and working children will arise from work with targeted communities. This could entail improvements to health and welfare, adult literacy, employment or income generation possibilities. However, it is important that the effects of these interventions on children are monitored. It is not sufficient to assume that improving the situation of women, for example, will automatically improve the lives of children. It may even make children's lives worse. Likewise, water and sanitation projects do not always have entirely positive effects for children. One example illustrates both these points. In order to decrease women's work and improve water supply in a rural area a project replaced wells with pumps. As only one person at a time can use a pump, people had to queue for water. This meant that water collection took longer, so women sent children to do this. Indeed they sent the youngest children, who could be spared from other tasks. So younger children had to carry heavier loads.

Communities need to become aware of the special needs of children and accustomed to listening to children's points of view. Project planning for development should take into account the perspectives of all community members, not only men and women, but also children and young people.

A distinction can be made between projects that work with children and those that work with communities. This overlaps with the division between service providing and development projects. Service provision not only creates dependency, but also treats children as if they are separate from communities.

Of course, they *may* be separated from their communities of origin and from their families, at least on a temporary basis. However, they come from communities, and, wherever they live, they are close to communities – in them but not of them.

Tobias Hecht, who has studied street children in Recife, Brazil, says that, from the window of his apartment, he could see the activities of a local group of street children. There was a place where they slept, a swimming pool they used after hours by climbing the perimeter wall, a restaurant where they could get food, a daily breakfast for the first three to arrive at a particular house, a place where they could wash their clothes and, of course, places to beg or earn money. Even though they did not live in houses, and came from other places, they interacted with members of this community.

CHILDREN IN DEVELOPMENT

... children are almost never involved in the planning of projects and are rarely even consulted. In some countries they are not seen as having any special needs or, indeed, any rights. It is important not to be complacent about the likely effects of a development programme on their lives. It is, in fact, evident that the very process of development and the social and economic transformations that have accompanied it has harmed many children.

Children should take priority in all development initiatives because an investment in the wellbeing of the child is an investment in the future of the community as a whole (Oxfam, *Field Directors' Handbook*, p51).

National and international advocacy

Local level awareness-raising is an important part of community development. However, there are larger arenas in which advocacy of children's rights in general, and the situation of street and working children in particular, are important. Much depends on the national situation of children, about which you will have learned in the first part of your research. Advocacy is likely to concentrate both on general children's rights and on specific issues affecting street and working children. Although general public awareness is important, the target groups for this work are likely to be:

* government departments;
* police and legal services;
* education departments and schools;
* employers;
* trades unions;
* health departments and health personnel.

The main focus for this work now is reporting to the United Nations Committee on the Rights of the Child, to which most countries are committed. The role of

NGOs in this is important, and in many countries they have developed coalitions for children's rights and are involved in the reporting process, sometimes writing alternative reports for the Committee. Your project will be most effective if it is involved in such a coalition, rather than 'going it alone'.

INSTITUTIONAL RESPONSES

The institutional solution for street children that has been used historically and still predominates in most countries is some kind of residential setting, a school, an orphanage or a reformatory. Many children find themselves virtual prisoners in these closed environments even if they are not actually put into prison. In too many cases they are treated as delinquents and imprisoned with adults.

However benevolent an institution may be, it is now recognised by childcare experts that it is not the ideal solution. Children fail to learn the full range of social and emotional skills they will need as adults. It is impossible for them to be treated as individuals and unlikely that they will be able fully to develop their human potential. Institutions are also not cost-effective. They can take only a limited number of children and are expensive to run.

CHILDREN'S VIEWS OF INSTITUTIONS

Our findings reveal that among the ones that have been institutionalised some have been in observation/remand homes as many as four or five times and many children have expressed their aversion and negative feelings for these oppressive institutions that merely end up making 'criminals' out of innocent children.

... Also, street children, used to being outdoors, resist closed and strictly structured institutions which seem oppressive and prison-like to them and therefore often run way from them. One of the reasons why children are on the streets is to escape the confines of their overcrowded homes and therefore they do not want to trade this for the confines of an institution (Reddy, 1992, p98).

Closed institutions are the option generally preferred by governments and municipal authorities, as well as religious and traditional NGOs. This is a tidy solution as it cleans the streets and the children. People who provide funds, including many donor organisations, are satisfied with the image of a washed child, with clean clothes, elementary schooling, a plate of food and a mug. Children often wear uniforms and live regimented lives. Education is usually limited to provision of basic skills, which are typically carpentry and electrical wiring for boys and sewing and typing for girls. Many of the children in orphanages are not even orphans.

It is difficult to wean some donors, especially local business benefactors, away from the idea of institutional responses. One reason is that they are hooked on the idea of rescue. In addition, charity is rarely free. Donors want something back, whether this is their name on a plaque or minibus, a photograph of a building or of smiling children for the office wall. Donors like to be able to visit, and to show other people round. They want visible results from their charitable investment, and want to be able to quote the numbers of children who have successfully graduated as carpenters (regardless of whether or not they may have found employment). It is far more difficult to get them to invest in something less tangible.

So donors need educating, and you may have to do this by, for example, demonstrating to both donors and government agencies that alternatives work (and are more cost-effective). This is an important part of the NGO role.

You also need to be clear about the disadvantages of institutional responses (some for the children, some for the donors):

- Institutionalisation of children – they fail to learn social skills, such as shopping, washing their own clothes; or to develop the social skills of making decisions or forming emotional relationships with particular adults.
- Children fail to develop their potential, which is a loss not only to them but also to the community and nation.
- Institutions are not cost-effective.
- They deal with small numbers of children and leave the larger problems unresolved.
- They ignore children's coping skills and networks.
- They may institutionalise children who are not orphans and ignore their families.
- They stigmatise children as different from the rest of the community and recipients of charity, especially if they have to wear uniforms.
- They may ultimately criminalise children who 'escape' the regimentation to the freedom of the streets.

'NON-INSTITUTIONAL' RESPONSES

During the last two decades, some alternatives have been tried that claim to be non-institutional. They emphasise the importance of going out on to the streets and into the workplaces where the children are to be found, respecting their autonomy and skills and listening to their points of view.

In the typical 'non-institutional' model, which was developed in Latin America, children are contacted and befriended by 'street educators' (see page 134), who may provide certain services, such as first aid or health care, on the street, but encourage children to visit an open facility, such as a drop-in centre, where a variety of activities are possible, including provision of meals, washing facilities, counselling and recreation, as well as some protected work opportunities.

These projects are able to work with a large number of children and the facilities cost far less to run than closed institutions. Over the years certain projects have become world famous and many of their experiences have been reproduced in other places. However, they remain fundamentally focused on service provision and, despite decades of work, not one project has decreased the number of street and working children in its local area.

The term 'non-institutional' is also technically incorrect, particularly in the case of those projects that eventually take children off the streets and into a residential setting, which is what many aim to do. These are very organised, often extremely large agencies with internal rules and quite rigid structures; in other words, they are definitely institutions. But by using the term 'non-institutional' they distance themselves from the traditional orphanages and reformatories and signal the fact that they try to respect children's perspectives and rights.

The project options discussed below are all taken from the experiences of projects that would describe themselves as 'non-institutional' (for in-depth consideration of alternatives to institutional care, see Tolfree, 1995).

SERVICE PROVISION OR DEVELOPMENT?

SERVICE PROVISION CREATES DEPENDENCY

Giving food and blankets for a long time might give a distorted idea of what we want them to do. If we start with a few of them, the next day we will be confronted by an army of children 'desperately' in need of help This way we encourage them to beg. They already do it and don't learn anything new. We spoil them since we make them think that 'being poor and in tattered clothes' is a way to earn money. We know that in some countries begging has become big business. The children on the street know this as well. Is this what we want to impress upon them? ...

Be cautious in presenting yourself as 'Father Christmas' with your hands full of gifts. Nothing is free in life and they know it. They experience it daily. Don't put them in a world of [your] dreams (Dallape, 1988, pp23 and 51).

In work with street children, and to a certain extent with working children, there is a tendency for projects to concentrate on providing services – food, health care, shelter and education. The soup kitchen and the orphanage, both nineteenth century solutions, are seldom far from people's minds when they think of homeless and working children. But giving handouts of various kinds is only a short-term solution, a kind of first aid. And it can create dependency.

On the other hand, it is not possible to direct project activities only towards development and prevention. You cannot ignore children who are in danger, frightened, hungry or ill because development philosophy says you should look for long-term solutions. In a sense, street and working children are in a permanent emergency or disaster-relief situation. As in the case of earthquake victims and refugees, they need immediate help, but this will be of maximum benefit to them if it is planned so that it will become part of a long-term development solution.

TYPES OF SERVICE PROVISION

In the crisis situations faced by many street and working children, service provision may well be a key element of any project. This chapter provides an overview, with some examples, of the most common types of provision.

Shelters and drop-in centres

Shelters create alternative environments for children whose lives are difficult. They are places where children can feel relaxed and comfortable, safe and looked after. They are not places for regimentation, hierarchy and authority. They are places where children can talk to each other and to project workers, knowing they will be both listened to and heard. They are not places where they will be talked at or preached to, even though they should be places where they may be able to practice, learn or recover the skills and habits of good interpersonal relationships. Shelters should not resemble remand homes or orphanages, where children say they feel like prisoners.

Night shelters
One major decision faced by many projects is whether or not to provide a night shelter. It is at night that children experience the greatest dangers on the street, but some programmes provide shelter at drop-in centres only during daylight hours. There are several reasons for this:
- night shelters become like orphanages or remand homes, and create dependency;

- many children do have homes to return to;
- shelter can only be given to relatively small numbers of children, whereas drop-in centres can provide for larger numbers;
- if a shelter has to be staffed by project workers at night this increases the wage bill, especially as live-in night work often has to be paid at a higher rate than day-time work. Some projects compromise by using untrained staff, such as watchmen, at night, which means lower wages. Others argue that it is during the hours of darkness that disturbed children suffer their greatest loneliness, fear and unhappiness. This is when they are most vulnerable, and most in need of professional caring and counselling.

On the other hand, in some situations, such as in recent years in South Africa, the dangers on the streets from vigilantes, police or society's own conflicts make it imperative to provide a safe haven for children both day and night. Where the children's safety is under this kind of threat the sort of shelter that is provided may look like a closed institution, but this is less to keep the children in than to keep society out!

WHAT IS A SHELTER?

The objectives of ... a shelter are to provide safety, security, health care, nutrition and education for the street child without encouraging the child to become dependent either on the shelter or the organisation that runs it. People responsible for this kind of shelter must closely interact with the street child. They must create situations where such children can come together and get the attention they badly need: they must also strengthen and constructively direct their independence, while encouraging interdependence (Pattabhirama Reddy of The Concerned for Working Children, in *Molaké*, Vol 2 No 2, 1992, p3).

What do shelters provide?

Shelters may provide:
- storage facilities for working materials, clothes, personal belongings and money;
- washing facilities for clothes and bodies;
- an opportunity for rest;
- sleeping facilities;
- recreation and play opportunities;
- food and/or cooking facilities;
- meals;

- health services;
- health education;
- sheltered work opportunities;
- education;
- skills training;
- counselling.

What standard of shelter is required?

One of the most common mistakes made by people planning street children projects is the assumption that a purpose-built, or specially adapted, centre must be found before work can begin. This means a good deal of money has to be raised, and the fundraising efforts and search for property can take over the whole project, meaning that little or no work goes in to contact with children or finding out what their needs really are.

There are also a good many projects for street children that consist of more or less well-equipped buildings, used by very few children. This may be because the building is not in a good part of town for the children – it is too far away from where they work, for example. It is also likely that the children do not know of its existence, because the project has never really made contact with them. Or it may be that the services provided are not appropriate.

You will remember the example of SABANA's Drop In Center at the top of Smokey Mountain. The project went to where the children worked, made use of a disused building, observed the children until it was sure of one of their immediate needs – drinking water – and provided it: 'Slowly children began to drift in to drink and wash their hands and, as they finally became familiar with the staff, to talk' (Gunn & Ostos, 1992, p633).

Another solution is to make use of unused or borrowed spaces. The Khar Danda YMCA in Bombay made use of unused time in its centre to start a street children project. The building was used for adult training classes between nine in the morning and nine at night. During the night hours when it would otherwise have been empty, the project used the building as a shelter. Project Alternatives in Honduras uses a variety of borrowed spaces throughout the capital city, Tegucigalpa: rooms in the commercial market places for feeding and education programmes, 'free time' in a municipal medical centre, extra spaces in other street children projects for children with particular problems. This avoids expensive overheads, makes sure that resources are maximised and not duplicated, and ensures a city-wide spread of activities.

Whatever a shelter provides, it should be in keeping with the way in which people in the surrounding community live. Unfortunately, many donors, especially from the developed world, like to see photographs of high quality accommodation and may build centres that seem luxurious to the local community. This can further separate street children from the community. People in Romania, for example, stigmatise street children even more since Western European generosity has provided some centres for them that far surpass the living conditions of families struggling to survive.

This does not mean that there are no standards of provision for street children. They need somewhere to go that they can be proud of and that makes them feel they are worth something. But simple accommodation is best. They can also be encouraged to use or develop skills in building, decorating and maintaining 'their' centre.

FINDING A NAME FOR A STREET CHILDREN'S PROJECT IN SRI LANKA

Attempting to build on the children's yearning for an identity, we felt it was a good idea to involve them in finding a name and perhaps an emblem for our centre. [We asked them] to explain what they did when they were at the centre. It emerged very quickly that they thought of it as a school. As the discussion continued, it became more and more clear that the concept 'school' was very important to them. That is where other children went every day and this was THEIR school ... Several names came out of this process ... Several felt that 'Joseph's school' was a good idea. It is the name of an established and famous secondary school in Colombo ... Other suggestions were 'Poor Children's School' and 'School for Children who have no Home' ... The last two names met with fervent objections from some of the older boys who insisted that the name didn't have to say they had no home!

The proposal that finally won the vote was 'United Children's School'. We should add that the concept, united, has little to do with a romantic unification of street children. There is a United Soccer Club ... The use of the word, united, can be seen on billboards ranging from United Motors to United Industries and United Printers ... The most important outcome of this process was that the youth had established for themselves that they attend a school – not a centre or a street children project (What's Inside?, 1989, pp45-6).

Where should a shelter be?

Wherever possible, shelters and other project centres should be located within communities, ideally those from which the children come. The SCF programme in San Pedro Sula, Honduras, found that, while a drop-in centre in the central market served a purpose for children, it actually isolated them and made them different, leading to further stigmatisation. Local communities can protest at first that they do not want a centre for 'criminal children' in their backyard, but over time they can accept and even help the project. If the centre is located in the children's own community it can become a multi-purpose facility, not just limited to street and working children. It can open educational and counselling services to other children and families, which reduces the stigmatisation and envy and also serves the purpose of reaching children who may be at risk of leaving home or dropping out of school. It can provide the means by which service provision becomes community development work.

THIS IS OUR HOME

... the decision on who enters [the shelter] rests with the boys. With several visitors coming to photograph and talk to the boys, the boys feel that sometimes they do not want to talk about themselves. In such instances the boys have decided to reject talking or posing for normal photos.

This decision is in fact based on the issue of the privacy of the child. Very often people enter a street child's life, asking personal questions and expecting to receive answers. And they do not volunteer any information about their own lives (YUVA, 1992, pp17-18).

Food

Giving food to orphan children is inevitably linked with the pathetic image of Oliver Twist. Too often food is distributed as an act of regimented charity for which children are made to feel grateful and is of very basic quality and dubious nutritional value. Many street children are not hungry, they are able to buy their own food from their own income or to beg reasonable food from restaurants. It all depends on local conditions and prior research should reveal what food needs children may have.

One group often ignored in food provision is children at work. Employers may not object to food being brought by the project to the workplace, as well-fed workers are more productive. Self-employed children in street trades may welcome a cheap alternative to fast food and stalls providing meals for adult workers. In both cases, a minimum charge avoids creating dependency and respects the children's independence.

Working children living with their families are likely to have greater needs for food than street children, especially if they are girls. Indeed girls working at housework and childcare so that their mothers can go out to work are likely to be far more in need of food supplements than their working brothers or children living outside families on the street.

If at all possible, it is worth researching nutritional status for your target groups of children.

FOOD: THE CHILDREN'S PERCEPTION

We like a centre where the FOOD is good
We do not like a centre
— where the food is fit to be eaten only by pigs
— where the meals are served late
— where the food is not enough
— where not getting food is used as punishment
— where the food for the staff is much better than that for the children.
(Street Children in Asia, 1989, p18)

Learning about nutrition

A far better option than food handouts is to instill good nutritional habits. Teaching about nutrition affects not only the children themselves but also their parents and, later on, their own children. And this includes not just learning about proteins, fats and carbohydrates but also about shopping, food preparation and storage. Too many projects employ a cook to provide a daily meal for children without making full use of this resource and the space given over to the kitchen. Use the cook and the kitchen as teaching resources, integrate them into the project. Children can learn to shop, cook and clear up – skills they may never have learned at home.

Meal-times, as the staff of the Redd Barna (Norwegian Save the Children) project in Sri Lanka point out, can also be the focus of learning about nutrition. According to Redd Barna policy, posters are displayed in the dining area, showing:
- body-building foods (proteins);
- energy foods (carbohydrates);
- protective foods (vitamins and minerals).

The children check at each meal that all three types of food are included. Meal-times are also a socialisation process, as the project staff put it, 'Eating is a very intimate social act. It is the ritual of sharing food and soul' (What's Inside?, p53). During these daily social events children see their own behaviour mirrored in the behaviour of others, learn to adapt and learn to share.

The cost of food

One aspect in which projects differ is whether or not food is free, or children have to pay. Many projects argue that street and working children know only too well that nothing is free in this world, and will not value free handouts. They claim that providing free meals creates dependency and lessens the children's self-esteem. In order to maintain the children's dignity many projects charge a nominal or symbolic amount for food. Project Alternatives charges each of the undernourished market children it feeds daily the small sum of 5 lempiras, which is well within the family budget.

In Redd Barna's Sri Lanka project the decision was taken to charge the meals at cost, covering the price of ingredients but not the cook's wages. Only milk is free, although meals are provided at no cost during emergencies and curfews when children cannot work. Staff report that children are well aware of the cost of food and appreciate the need to purchase goods in bulk to keep costs low. They advise staff to buy with care and also do some of the shopping themselves: 'They keep account of the amount, cost, change and quality of the produce, reporting back to the teachers' (What's Inside?, p51). Everything can become a learning experience!

Health

From worldwide reports, Unicef Health Promotion Unit has derived a list of the main physical illnesses from which street children suffer:
- respiratory problems, ranging from coughs and bronchitis to tuberculosis;
- skin infections;
- injuries, from fights, traffic accidents and other daily dangers;
- stomach worms and other intestinal parasites;
- sickness, diarrhoea and other stomach problems;
- kidney and bladder infections;
- bad teeth;
- sexually transmitted diseases, including HIV/Aids;
- eye infections, especially conjunctivitis.

(Connolly, 1994)

They may also be users of drugs – cigarettes, alcohol, glue and other substances. In addition, they may be suffering from a range of psychological problems, depression and suicidal feelings.

Children do not know how to protect themselves from what are in many cases quite simple illnesses. They do not have the means to cure or protect themselves, they do not have control over their bodies, because they do not have correct information about illness or about their own bodies.

Working children also suffer from many of these common ailments, but are probably more likely to be malnourished, and may have a variety of complaints that are the result of poor working conditions. There is very little hard information about this, and your own researches in this area may well provide useful information for bodies such as the ILO. Among the most common effects of hazardous working conditions are:

- skin, eye and respiratory infections due to dust;
- eye damage from working at intricate tasks in poor light;
- hearing damage due to excessive noise;
- damage to physical growth because of working in fixed positions and awkward postures, combined with injuries from repetitive tasks, heavy work and using tools designed for adults;
- body, nerve and brain damage from exposure to toxic substances.

It is worth remembering that working conditions that would be hazardous for adults are likely to be far more dangerous to the developing minds and bodies of children.

For both street and working children the provision of health services is twofold, emergency help first, then developmental work, both of which can be activities in which children learn to help themselves.

First aid services

First aid and immediate health care should be provided on the streets or at the workplace, including training for the children in first aid and primary health care. This should be non-judgemental and free, and can be provided by outreach workers trained in the use of a simple medical kit.

Providing a health clinic at the project centre is not generally as effective as this friendly, easy to use outreach work. As prevention is better than cure, the centre is better advised to provide facilities where children can wash, and eat clean food, as well as learn how to protect themselves from disease and treat simple ailments. The YUVA project in Bombay has provided a first aid box at the night shelter. After training, it is in the children's hands, encouraging them to take responsibility for their own bodies.

If the centre has resources for a clinic to which more serious cases can be referred by the outreach workers, it should operate at hours that suit the children rather than the staff. It may be better if doctors and nurses do not wear uniforms. It is also helpful to have made contact with local clinics and hospitals so that an arrangement for in-patient referrals exists before an emergency arises. Many hospitals refuse (at first) to treat street and working children. In addition you will find that many children will not wish to go to hospital; they may have had experience of rough treatment already or heard of friends who have been turned away. They are likely to be afraid:

- of doctors;
- of procedures;
- of insults;
- that they will be left to die because they belong to no one, so that their bodies/organs will be sold.

Developmental health care

Health care provision must be backed up with, or develop into, health education. The best method for this is not to call in health care experts to give talks but to design a long-term programme that is integrated into other activities. Health is a life style issue. That is why staff at the Undugu programme in Kenya suggest the following first steps:

- Look at how the children live from a health point of view. Where, with whom and how do they live, sleep and eat? What do they eat and drink? Are they using alcohol, cigarettes and other substances?
- How do they describe their own health problems? Ask them to recall their illnesses and injuries over the past month and describe the symptoms. Find out what words they use for different illnesses and parts of the body. How do they think their bodies work?

On the basis of this, start a participatory health education programme (including parents and communities where you can, but using the children as health educators). Use group discussion, song, dances and drama. Children can make puppets and 'write' their own plays and draw their own educational posters.

- Emphasise that prevention is better than cure and that almost all their illnesses can be prevented.
- Emphasise that cure is nearly always best achieved by simple means. Few diseases need the heavy treatment of modern drugs. Find out about these simple treatments, such as oral rehydration therapy for diarrhoea.
- Buy a copy of the health care manual, *Where there is no doctor* (described in the further reading chapter), and use it, don't just put it on the shelf. If they can read English (or Spanish), make sure the children know about it and use it too.
- Start from children's own health problems as they state them.
- Don't be judgemental.
- Don't get in doctors and nurses to give talks to the children and assume the job is done, or show videos and think the task is complete. Experts and other resources from outside are only useful in the context of a participatory health education programme.

- Help the children to understand their own bodies and take responsibility for their health and the health of those around them.
- Demonstrate good habits yourselves. If the project has a 'no smoking' rule this applies to staff and visitors. And don't allow visitors to give children sweets (if they must give handouts, fruit is better).

FLEXIBLE HEALTH EDUCATION

When Undugu first started the programme on health, the health staff team provided services from 9 to 12 every morning, except Saturdays and Sundays. After a period of time, almost all the participants in the health programme left. The team tried to find out why the people were not interested in their training. Were their lessons boring? Or were the people not sufficiently motivated? None of these reasons were true; the timetable was wrong. For street children and, for different reasons, for slum dwellers, a timetable doesn't work. As stated earlier, their understanding of discipline is different from ours. It is therefore important:

- that they set their own timetable to make sure that this does not interfere with other important activities, like their working hours, cinemas etc;
- that the time spent should be short and full of action;
- to stop immediately if you see that the participants are not interested; and
- to be flexible, creative and imaginative in changing the environment and selecting places. You need space to move, play, laugh and dance (Dallape 1988, p67).

Special health problems – sexually transmitted diseases and substance abuse

Although they are not numerically the most important, two specific problems affecting many street children that cause concern for many projects are substance abuse and sexually transmitted diseases, including HIV infection. In both cases, of course, prevention is better than cure and education about both issues should be integrated into the overall health education programme, which should include sexual education. It is not enough to show the occasional video, lecture about the dangers of drugs and HIV, or hand out condoms. Substance abuse and sexuality are complex issues. The majority of children on the street are at an age when both topics should be openly discussed in a non-judgemental way. For this to be possible it is important for adult project workers to be able to discuss these topics openly and to be well-informed. This area of health education starts with educating yourselves. This is where the maxim that the main barrier is your own attitudes becomes particularly relevant.

The main problem project workers have when thinking about sexually transmitted diseases, including HIV infection and Aids, is that, according to the Western image of childhood, children are not supposed to be involved in sexual relationships. The fact of life on the streets is that many are involved in sex as casual prostitutes (both boys and girls), through rape and assault by adults or older children, and in relationships with each other. Project workers need to be realistic about this and to question their own attitudes.

Children do need to be protected from assault and from infection, not only from HIV but also from other sexually transmitted diseases. In the first case they may need actual physical protection (but not incarceration). In the second they should be able to protect themselves through knowledge about infection and treatment and probably access to condoms.

There is nothing to be gained from judgemental attitudes that make children feel bad about themselves and their developing sexuality. If an intimate relationship with another street child, be it heterosexual or homosexual, has been an experience of affection and warmth this should not be condemned. All too often street children projects think that all they have to do is take a child off the streets and away from 'temptation' and all will be well. In one religious foundation in Colombia the technique was to make sure that boys had no 'dark places' available where they could indulge in sexual activities. If they persisted they were given sex instruction and exposed to 'positive models' of women, which meant nurses and teachers. Clearly such a blinkered approach and narrow definition of sexuality and gender roles would be of little use in helping children develop secure sexual identities.

Unfortunately, many project workers and management teams would rather not confront children's needs and are satisfied to ignore them or sit them down in front of a video from time to time. However, some projects and agencies have developed their own information and resource packs for HIV and sex education. These are of varying quality and are best used interactively with your own project, adapting them to local conditions. Lists of sources of information are given at the end of this manual.

One factor to be aware of when choosing resources for HIV education is that street children are not impressed by messages that stress the danger of Aids. They already live violent, dangerous lives, and are more interested in the business of survival than in a relatively far-off illness or invisible threat. Ana Filgueiras, who works with street girls in Brazil, suggests, 'If you tell them Aids makes you very weak, that's something they're afraid of. They know that when they're weak they can't survive on the street.'

In any case, prevention of HIV infection is much more than a matter of safe sex messages and condom use. It is concerned with children's total development. Thus prevention is integral to the entire project because:

- a child who has an income or economic support will not sell sex for money;
- a child who can count on adequate food will not sell sex for a meal;
- a child who does not take drugs will not sell sex for the next high;
- a child who knows about the way bodies work is more likely to take an interest in his or her own health;
- a child whose health is good will be less likely to become infected with HIV;
- a child whose health is good will be less likely to develop Aids if he or she does become HIV positive;
- a child who is developing skills through education and vocational training is more likely to feel good about his or herself and positive about the future;
- a child who has opportunities to talk about bad experiences with an understanding counsellor is likely to develop a better self image;
- a child who feels good about his or herself is more likely to take preventative measures in sex, as for health in general.

The most successful HIV prevention work is thus part of the project as a whole.

In contrast to the tendency of projects to leave sexual subjects alone, substance abuse often attracts a good deal of attention, much of it misguided. Use of alcohol, nicotine and marijuana are often seen as 'normal' by the children. You need to find out what they regard as addictive or bad substances. There is usually a clear distinction between drug addicts and non-drug users on the street. Street children know that they need to be alert and can despise those who become incapable of rational action because of drug use. They will often tell project workers to keep away from those 'bad' people. But sometimes they will, for a variety of reasons, go on a bender on some substance or other. Other children are clearly damaged by and addicted to a variety of substances. However, it is worth noting that, as in the case of HIV, 'Programmes *without* the "fight against drugs" label tend to work better, providing more options and alternatives' (Connolly, 1994).

The problem is that there is little expertise in the area of detoxification for children, and few options and alternatives available. Little or nothing is known about the effects of different substances on children at various ages, as opposed to adults. There is almost no expertise in working with child substance abusers, and it is unlikely to be available where your project is based. This is a job for experts, but none exist. The frustrations will be enormous.

The solution adopted by YUVA in Bombay was to give up working with the heavy substance abusers and instead lobby for their care:

It must be understood that until such time that proper, continuous and appropriate after-care is ensured to a street child, any attempts at coercing children to giving up drugs are in fact harmful to children. This is because the children are totally demotivated to bear the effort and pain they go through during the detoxification treatment, when they know that they will be back on the streets and (most likely) into drugs again (YUVA, p10).

This is a point worth considering. What your project has to think about in the case of heavy substance users, as opposed to educating others about substance use, is whether or not they are part of the target group and if working with them is appropriate within the project objectives. You have to consider whether or not you have the capacity and skills for this work, and to use contacts within the local area to find out if there are any suitable programmes to which you may be able to refer children, if they are willing. YUVA took a courageous and difficult decision. Your project will have to take its own, in the light of resources and local conditions. Above all it is important not to overstretch project staff by undertaking specialist work for which they have no training, expertise or resources.

Education

Children are expected to be in schools, and thus education tends to be a major component of projects with street and working children. This may target:
- working children with no schooling;
- working school drop-outs;
- working children who are falling behind at school;
- potential school drop-outs;
- new school enrollees;
- youth, for basic skills of numeracy and literacy and some vocational training.

WHAT IS LITERACY FOR?

Little street girl: I would like to read.
Community worker: Would you like to read books?
Little street girl: No, I would like to read the shining lights over the shops.
(in Summing Up, 1990, p6)

Formal and non-formal education
The terms used to describe educational project work can be confusing. Although the education provided by projects is often referred to as 'non-formal', this usually only entails a contrast with the formal state system of schooling. It is not a comment on the methods used, which are often every bit as formal as those of state schools, with blackboards, authoritarian teachers and children sitting in rows. It is better

to think of the education provided in projects as complementary to the state system. However, it is preferable if alternative methods of learning and teaching are employed.

Basic education

Another term that is much in vogue is 'basic education', which was confirmed as a right for all individuals at the World Conference on Education for All in Jomtien, Thailand, in 1990 (WCEFA, 1990).

Basic education encompasses both *tools* of literacy, numeracy and problem-solving and *content*, such as knowledge, values and attitudes.

United Nations agencies, such as Unicef and Unesco, are working to implement the Declaration made at Jomtien, most particularly through the Goals for Children in the 1990s adopted in the same year at the World Summit for Children. In addition to increased pre-school education, better education for girls, reduction of adult literacy and increasing the knowledge levels of the population in general, the goal most important for street and working children is:

> Universal access to basic education, and achievement of primary education by at least 80 per cent of primary school-age children through formal schooling or non-formal education of comparable learning standard ...

Some education systems have developed programmes for non-formal education to complement school-based learning and many projects make use of the materials developed. Non-formal education classes are held when children are able to attend, at the end of the working day, at weekends or other holiday times. The classes are genuinely free, whereas so much state schooling entails hidden costs of uniforms, books and registration. They also often include other services, such as giving a meal or at least a snack (it is very hard to concentrate and learn if you are hungry). If non-formal education takes place outside normal school hours it may be able to make use of existing school buildings. Teachers may be volunteers, often based in the local community.

Teaching and learning methods

However, not all street and working children are able to benefit from these programmes, which are essentially formal in methods. They need more participatory ways of learning, particularly in the early stages. Teacher training tends not to include these alternative methods and this means that teachers employed by projects may only be comfortable with formal ways of teaching. These may be unsuitable for children whose time and energy are limited and whose concentration span is short.

TRYING TO TEACH STREET CHILDREN

The volunteers were filled with enthusiasm. Thinking that 'work with them' could only mean 'teach them', the volunteers went back and built a blueprint of action geared towards education. They decided to attack the problems of the street children with an armory of pencils, slates, books – the instruments of teaching.

... Only about 3-4 boys attended 'classes' and the others watched. This went on for about 10 days, during which the volunteers had to bear with extreme rudeness, violent swearing and spitting and also some beatings.

It took a lot of introspection and determination on the part of the volunteers to decide, finally, that they must go on. Becoming one with the boys, gaining their trust and friendship almost became an obsession for the volunteers. It took six months for the results of their efforts to show. But a lot happened in these six months. There were brawls, bash-ups, animosities and also changes. Changes – slow but positive. There were changes in the boys, in our goals, in the volunteers' outlook and in the process itself (YUVA, p4).

Education for street and working children should start from where they are and be based on the kinds of experiences they have:

- It does not have to be classroom-based. You do not need purpose-built premises, although don't turn down any offer of loaned space. Project Alternatives, working in Honduran market places, uses rooms provided by market owners. The children come for brief lessons still wearing their market aprons, and many bring smaller children that they have to care for. Many other projects get the chance to use school or community rooms out of school hours. The main thing is that the space should be convenient for the children; they should not have to travel long distances or be away from their workplace for long. In any case, you don't necessarily need a classroom. Child Workers in India has persuaded some employers to allow children to have classes on the work premises (it is better for employers to have employees with skills). Pavement schools are common in India. There is no reason why the street or a field should not be a learning environment. It is worth remembering that the word 'pedagogy' is derived from the Greek word for foot, just like pedestrian. Teachers used to walk about followed by their pupils.

- Timetables need to be really flexible, and particularly to take into account the hours children need to work. Even apparently free children of the street have their own timetables: traffic rush hours when they have to go and sell or beg to motorists, times when they go and collect left-over food from restaurants, for example. They can't be expected to give up these activities, which are essential for their survival, just to come to classes.

- Learning materials need to be adapted to the children's age and experience. No 14-year-old working child will be encouraged to read by using books intended for five-year-old, middle-class children. They need materials adapted to their interests and the things they know about. Cinemas, street life, the workplace and so on, things they are familiar with and words they use every day will be the things they will want to read about.

- The same goes for mathematics. They will already know how to count money, but they can learn more about how numbers can work for them – for example, through cooperative buying or savings accounts, or calculating their own profit and loss accounts.

- Best of all, the children can make their own books, or other learning materials such as wall newspapers to communicate with each other. They can start with pictures they cut from magazines, explaining to each other why they have chosen them. Perhaps they could chose a theme first. Then discussion of the pictures follows. Then they paste them on to sheets of paper and either they or the teacher can write a few words or a caption.

- One of the most useful aspects of the children making their own picture books, posters or wall newspapers in this way is that they can use the discussion to find out about their own lives: why they have to work, why others do not. For example, a picture of street children bathing in a fountain can lead to a discussion of why poor people in general do not have access to clean water supplies, or of the importance of hygiene, or of the requirement of government to provide services, such as water, to its citizens. This has two advantages:

  (i) Children begin to understand why they live the lives they do, which is the first step towards changing them. In this way education becomes an empowering process.

  (ii) They begin to understand that the reasons why they have to work, or are living on the streets, are due to social structures, not to their own mistakes or inadequacies. In this way education becomes a step in improving self-esteem.

- In this kind of education, traditional teaching in which teachers instruct passive children is no good at all. Teachers cannot come prepared into the classroom with a fixed curriculum and set books. They are facilitators, who help children come to a greater understanding of a world they already know, by providing opportunities, helping with skill development and following a curriculum set by the children and their lives. The process is one of learning rather than teaching.

- This type of learning seldom takes place using 'chalk and talk' with children sitting quietly in rows, behind desks. It is often noisy and messy. It uses drama, song, puppets, mime, discussion, drawing, painting, modelling. It is fun. It is serious fun. It can lead to moments of intense concentration, quiet and reflection. The lessons learned are seldom forgotten.

- This type of learning is seldom taught in teacher training college (although there are usually some lecturers and many more students who know about it, and even practice it). To learn more about it read the books by Paulo Freire that have been adapted successfully by three generations of teachers with disadvantaged groups around the world. The most useful are *Literacy in 36 hours* and *The pedagogy of the oppressed*. For a practical example of the way it can be used with children, see *The child's language and the teacher* by Krishna Kumar (for details, see Appendix 3, p175).

- This type of learning can spread like wildfire around a community or within a group Who does not want to show someone else a book they have made, a poster they helped to make, or to have their friends come and see them in a play?

- Do not assume that all children who have dropped out of school have done so for economic reasons or because the curriculum is not relevant to their lives. Some will have done so because they have learning difficulties. These may be as easy to address as poor eyesight, where a place at the front of the class or a pair of spectacles will be all that is needed. Others might have more deep-rooted disabilities that require specialist help This is where you can call on expert advice and tests from education or psychology departments to find out which children are affected and what specialist remedial support they may require.

Relationships with the formal education system

Of course, you may have problems with officers of the Ministry of Education, but even there you will have sympathisers. And they may help you to systematise what you are doing so that it can be replicated in other projects or ask you to come and talk in a teacher training college.

In any case, even before you begin you should seek Ministry approval for your work, and find out if there is a non-formal education department, syllabus and materials. You also need to find ways in which children can graduate from your non-formal education to the formal education system, entering the grade that is correct for their age (few things can be more demoralising for a teenager than being put into a class of seven-year-olds). After children have re-entered the formal system they may well need to continue with the non-formal programme to support their progress and build their confidence further. In this way a non-formal system becomes complementary to the formal system, and can also help children who are falling behind in school and are at risk of dropping out.

Going beyond literacy and numeracy

Education for children who are on the fringes of society is not just a matter of reading, writing and arithmetic. Other non-formal education may include dealing with many of the following, all of which could prevent a child from entering, or being successful in, formal schools:

- social skills;
- emotional and physical self-control;
- attention;
- listening skills (and knowing when to be quiet);
- vague concepts of time and of age;
- poor memory and concentration;
- unclear spatial concepts;
- inability to classify: 'The children know names such as pumpkin, tomato, beef, chicken or chillie but not categories such as fruit, vegetable, meat and poultry' (What's Inside?, p38)
- poor motor skills – inability to hold and control a pencil, or fold paper neatly;
- poorly developed ideas of personal property (this can be a problem when it comes to which school books are 'yours' and 'mine');
- being unaccustomed to sitting (many prefer to kneel or stand to work);
- feelings of claustrophobia in rooms and buildings;
- poor knowledge and understanding of everyday culture;
- how to take care of their own bodies and clothing.

Children who live largely away from their families will have learned some social skills before they left home, but there are likely to be gaps in their behaviour and understanding. Redd Barna's Sri Lanka staff comment that 'It's like learning to say "Hello" but not having learned to say "Goodbye"' (What's Inside?, p14). The missing elements in each individual child's socialisation will not be immediately obvious, nor will they all be the same. Staff need to work with and observe the children over a long period of time and seize every moment and opportunity as a learning possibility.

LEARNING LIFE SKILLS IN A STREET CHILDREN PROGRAMME

Among other things, socialisation in the programme has concentrated on health, hygiene, table manners, clean and ironed clothes, an introduction to life cycle events such as births and weddings and explaining the appropriate behaviours required and significance attached to them, knowledge of public and religious holidays, the capacity to listen and learning to take simple responsibilities (What's Inside?, p15).

Vocational training

Vocational training is a common education option in projects for children over 14 years of age, although it is often accompanied by basic literacy and numeracy. Vocational training schemes are often run by government as well as by NGOs. As in institutions, they usually offer a restricted range of skills, such as carpentry and electrical wiring for boys and sewing and typing for girls. Quite apart from the low ceiling they place on children's opportunities and the way they stereotype boys and girls, they are seldom linked to the job market and many schemes do not either offer employment placements or follow up students to see if they are able to find work.

Vocational training schemes are of variable quality and usefulness even though, like orphanages, they present the public with the image of the type of project they think street children need. They are a neat 'solution' and usually find willing funders, often attracting money for decades without evaluation, let alone adaptation. If you consider vocational training as an option for your project, or are thinking about placing children in your project in a scheme run by another agency, you should ask yourself the following:

- Is the scheme based on market research? What skills are really needed on the local job market? Can the courses teach skills that can be adapted to meet changing employment opportunities?
- What courses are already available in the local area? Can your students attend these? Would they need to upgrade their reading and writing skills first? If so, then this should be the priority within your project and you may not need a vocational training scheme of your own.
- Will the course provide certificates that will help the students find work and give them a sense of achievement? Such certificates need to be

meaningful to employers and probably linked to a government scheme, not just something handed out at the end of the course.

- What literacy and numeracy skills do the children already possess? What does this imply for the balance between theory and practical work on the course?

- Students may need to be supported while they follow the course. How will their lost earnings be supplemented? Where will they live? What can be done to prevent them dropping out if some sudden crisis in their lives means that they have to find extra money? Will they need to buy materials for use during the course? How can they afford this?

- If the course is being run by another institution, will it accept street children as students? What will be their relationship with other students? Will they need to be provided with clothing, tools and materials?

- What can be done to help children find employment once they have graduated from the course? In some cases they will need to be provided with basic tool kits, perhaps through a loan scheme, in order to become self-employed. In others a pool of potential employers can be found, who will agree to take a percentage of ex-street children on their staff.

- Research to follow up the success of graduates of vocational training schemes is vital. If they are not finding work, you need to know why. Perhaps there are no openings for that kind of skill, in which case the course should be dropped in favour of another. Perhaps the skills are not appropriate for the particular market needs, so retraining may be necessary. Opportunities for upgrading skills should also be offered.

- Will the courses address individual differences in talent, motivation and interests? Before placing any child on a course, find out what he or she wants to do and is capable of; street and working children have as much right to career guidance as any other child. Don't assume that these children only have the potential for semi-skilled work for the rest of their lives. Callescuela, in Asunción, dreams of one day welcoming back its 'own' doctors and lawyers.

Recreation

Most projects offer some form of recreation, although this is often limited to a space for football or sport for boys. Recreation encompasses more than sport and is a necessity for girls and also for children with special needs, such as physical or mental disabilities.

Camping trips, visits and excursions all provide opportunities for children to learn about their society, have some respite from daily problems or drudgery and get to know project workers better. Visits may be brief and instructional, such as learning how to use a post office or visit a hospital, or they may be longer trips away to stay in the country or seaside.

WHAT'S INSIDE? LEARNING THROUGH EXCURSIONS

Whether it is the hesitant step outside the post office or the sturdy step into the hospital, the point is they are the first steps into the larger society. In our excursions and other events ... we have tried to create more opportunities for our children to experience the inside life of society. On excursions we make a point of visiting temples, museums or productive units. But it isn't always easy to get inside. There are gatekeepers at the doors and even when the children do their very best to look presentable, the gatekeepers may keep them outside. For street children, socialisation must ensure that both their social skills and their physical appearance must be minimally acceptable to society. Or the doors won't open (What's Inside?, p60).

In addition to enjoyment, the therapeutic and educational value of sport, visits, drama and art need to be maximised. Drama, for example, has the following advantages:

* learning to work as a group;
* learning skills of listening and responding;
* exercising restraint;
* speaking distinctly;
* waiting your turn;
* responsibility for others;
* memory tasks (learning 'lines');
* learning to be interactive rather than just reactive;
* expressing emotions safely;
* having fun;
* showing the world what you can do.

Recreation should be integrated into project planning and the children's development, rather than just a bit of fun on the side. Its effects should be monitored alongside other project components.

DEVELOPMENT WORK

Protected work opportunities

Rather than rescuing children from the street and the workplace, some projects acknowledge children's need to have an income and to respect their economic independence. The strategy these projects adopt minimises the risks of working by providing protected opportunities for earning money, either based on the child's current work or within a special working environment provided by the project.

In different parts of the world, projects have helped self-employed children to improve their working conditions by:

- providing a space where the work can take place, such as a car-wash scheme or shoeshine shop, where children will not be obliged to pay premiums to adult exploiters and where there is a guaranteed clientele;
- providing secure places where tools and goods can be kept overnight, or when the child is elsewhere;
- improving skills so that goods are better made or services provided more efficiently;
- registration schemes, combined with awareness campaigns, so that the public knows about the goods or services offered, have a guarantee of quality and know that the profits are for the children's benefit;
- help and training with business skills, through capital loans, cooperative purchasing and savings schemes.

Improving income

- The YMCA in Sorocaba helps shoeshiners to run their own cooperative. Polish and implements are bought in bulk and the children are able to work in a protected environment, as opposed to wandering the streets looking for custom in competition with adult shoeshiners with fixed posts who may chase them away. A shoeshine cooperative began with boys making the boxes they use to carry the polish, on which customers also rest their feet. These are sold for profit.
- Itinerant street sellers benefit enormously from the opportunity to buy in bulk and somewhere to keep their goods safely overnight or at times during the day when they are not selling (perhaps while they are in school). It is also possible for children to make goods for sale within the project. Thus postcards are sold to tourists in Cuzco and knick-knacks in Asunción, with labels indicating they are part of a street children scheme. This is also good public relations. In Asunción, project workers sometimes accompany child sellers to talk to purchasers about the children and the project.

- A car-wash scheme run in conjunction with a project can help in many ways. It takes away the high rates children often have to pay to 'rent' the piece of road they use (often from the porter of a building making a bit on the side, and also selling them water and taking money for storing the bucket and rags). It improves quality of service, it keeps the children away from negative influences such as older youths in informal car-wash lots who often use the service as an excuse to steal from cars.

Cooperatives

Children very frequently work in casual trades in which there is no job security, and working conditions and wages are not assured. Many children work for adults on the promise of pay they do not receive; all they get is a rain of blows to drive them away when they ask. They have no contract and no means of getting their rights. They are also in constant competition with each other, which further lowers wages and income. By forming cooperatives for mutual support, children can improve many of these things, and this, too, is a learning process about the need (and the ways) to work together successfully. Cooperatives and mutual work groups can be formed for any group of casual workers – newspaper sellers, car washers, ragpickers and cardboard collectors, children who help lorries load and unload in market places – you name it, it can be done.

Keeping money safe

Once income is improved, children need to have a safe place to keep their money. Some working children in street trades earn relatively large sums of money from time to time and have developed various ways of keeping it safe. Children who work in markets often develop a relationship with an adult stall-holder who acts as a banker. In Colombo, children sleep on the street with their money in their mouths. Another option is to spend all the money fast, often sharing with friends who will reciprocate when they in their turn are in funds. Jill Swart reports that the *malunde* (local name for street child) of South Africa keep mental accounts of intricate debt/ credit arrangements among themselves. This rapid spending of money gives the appearance of not wishing for anything other than short-term pleasure, but it really illustrates that there are practical obstacles to saving or making long-term plans. Banks would chase them away even if they knew how to open an account.

A savings scheme is at once a welcome service, a development mechanism and a learning process. The SCF project for working street children in San Pedro Sula, Honduras, operates a savings club for children in the central market. As in many other projects, the money from the savings scheme is then deposited in a joint account (called 'My Future') in a bank, where it earns interest. In some cases, parents are able to ask for, and obtain, loans on the security of their children's savings. Many projects with similar schemes hold weekly meetings at which children are made aware of how much they have saved, can check on the interest earned and decide on withdrawals to make purchases. Children themselves can run this type of bank committee.

Business schemes

A further option is for the project to develop its own business scheme. The SKI (Street Kids Incorporated) bicycle courier service is probably the best known of these. The original SKI project was established in Khartoum at a time when businesses and NGOs found it difficult to communicate with each other within the capital because of poor postal and telephone services. Children were trained in identifying street names, riding bicycles and road safety and given a bicycle and a uniform. SKI promised reliable, same day delivery. Children were given a salary, with bonuses for long distances and deductions for poor performance. If a bicycle went missing the boy had to pay.

On the surface this is a very attractive instant solution and this kind of scheme is attractive to donors. It aims to develop dignity and self-reliance, yet the very necessity to be businesslike means that there is a tendency to be authoritarian. SKI's own self-evaluation of its experience in Africa shows that children learn few skills and there is no community development, although this kind of project can be a helpful first step in a structured developmental programme for a child (Summing Up, 1990). For such a scheme to operate successfully, you need considerable start-up funding, as well as particular social conditions in which it would be financially and organisationally viable. It would be less successful, for example, in a larger city with better communications and heavier traffic.

Specific problems with this particular scheme illustrate the limitations of most instant-solution employment schemes which:

- require a well operating centre;
- require considerable start-up finance and organisation;
- require prior market research to see if goods/services will sell;
- target children who do not fit into other programmes easily;
- constitute an interim measure, not a solution – children should move on to other programmes that are more developmental;
- may break child labour laws and thus only be suitable for older children who have passed the minimum age for employment;
- can easily slide into being a youth employment scheme that does not cater for street children;
- may have to battle against public opinion that stigmatises street children and thus be unable to sell goods/services;
- expose children to hazardous traffic;
- may need equipment such as bicycles, which are valuable and could be stolen.

MAKING THE CHANGE FROM STREET LIFE TO A JOB, FROM JUST REACTING TO LIFE TO HAVING AN IDENTITY

Placing children in a situation where they are trained and employed on a regular basis does not automatically change their lifestyles. The gap between their unplanned, informal street activities and regular productive activities is a large one. The transformation process must take into account minute details and must move not just step by step, but inch by inch (SCF proposal for San Pedro Sula project, 1988).

Underlying principles

On the basis of his experience with the Undugu Society, Fabio Dallape urges projects to use realistic business principles to operate employment and savings schemes. Children should pay for the services they get from the project:

> Any improvements in their living conditions should be done by them with minimum inputs, if any from the agency. The group should appreciate the services we offer to them. Instil in them this sense of appreciation; they have to grow maintaining the sense of solidarity they have towards the poor. Make sure that they offer their services to others as soon as they receive them from us. This aspect is quite often neglected by us. We help them and are happy when some of them get employment or self-employment and we don't bother to verify how they behave with their friends who did not receive from us or from other agencies what they received (Dallape, 1988, pp49-50).

Disadvantages

The disadvantages of protected work schemes must be considered before selecting this option:
- there may be no market for the skills or services, or the market may not be able to bear expansion;
- follow-up is essential, it is not enough to find children a limited employment opportunity that sets a ceiling on their potential;
- the scheme will almost inevitably contravene child labour laws;
- goods and services must be real, not just a cover-up for charity;
- children need other opportunities to learn skills and knowledge for their futures;

- the scheme may create dependency, fail to tackle root causes and provide only short-term solutions;
- identifying children as street children in a protected work scheme may be stigmatising and may damage their self-image.

SCHEMES FOR GETTING AN INCOME

Profitable income generating projects are quite possible, but not easy to establish. Extensive prior training and supervision are required. Especially for collective enterprises, thorough organisational procedures with rules and regulations should be worked out with the children in advance. Such a procedure is in itself part of the socialisation process. In both individual and collective projects the issue of profitability is a major concern and the elementary principles of accounting should be taught. Like many poor in general, children would, for example, tend to disregard their own labour input as a cost in the production process (Summing Up, p27).

Working with communities

In community work you have first to define the community. This may be difficult in urban areas where local government administrative units may overlap or enclose different local groupings. Communities may live side by side, or be embedded in each other, with little or no intercommunication. An increasing problem in developing countries is that communities themselves may be subject to constant disruption. They are not the cosy units described by sociologists in the past; civil conflict and natural disasters are increasing everywhere, and communities are frequently divided, uprooted or ripped apart.

Communities – adults and children
Working with a community carries one major difficulty, which is that communities are dominated by adults who, in general, do not see children as an issue. Even when they are wanted, loved, perhaps indulged, noisy or troublesome, children are still to a very great extent invisible in the sense that their lives as children are taken for granted.

Community organisation is often left to those people who are most involved in day-to-day community life and networks within the community, which usually means the women. 'Parent groups', Tomas Andino of SCF Honduras says wryly, 'usually means mothers' groups.' The assumption then becomes that mothers' interests coincide with those of their children. To a certain extent this is true.

Women's organisations usually become involved in issues such as health care, potable water supplies and sanitation, all of which are undoubtedly good for children. However, issues that are specific to childhood, such as child abuse and exploitation, may not be addressed. This is where interventions that discuss the specific needs and interests of children as a group may be necessary. Although it is tempting to intervene by teaching adults about children, children's organisations (*of* rather than *for* children) may be the best way to make such an intervention.

Advantages and difficulties
The advantages of working with communities are:
- working with social groups that already exist, using their strengths, resources and values;
- not being limited to working with individual children;
- reaching a wider group of children, especially those at risk, and therefore having a preventative role;
- encouraging people, especially children, to look at the root causes of problems and find their own solutions;
- finding solutions that are viable within the economic and other resources of the community;
- economic sustainability and cost-effectiveness;
- not creating dependency;
- avoiding the creation of artificial categories of children, such as street children and child labourers, that stigmatise some groups and ignore other especially disadvantaged children;
- reducing the service provision role of projects;
- replicability – the principles can be used in other communities;
- a real development solution.

The difficulties of working with communities are that:
- it takes longer;
- it does not provide convenient photo opportunities for donors;
- it challenges staff and authorities to reconsider their ideas;
- it is difficult to get funding for initial stages;
- it does not clean the streets.

Children without community ties
When street children do not have family or community ties nearby, the obvious option may be to ignore any interactions they may have on a day-to-day basis with people who live in houses. These supports may seem too fragile, so a service centre may appear to be the most appropriate choice for project work. Nevertheless, Tomas Andino, of SCF's project for working children in San Pedro

Sula, Honduras, points out that providing a special centre for children can prevent community development by further separating children from possible interaction with the community in whose territory they live. It can stigmatise them. It also provides community members with a solution operated by an outside agency in which they are not involved. There are no structural changes and the project will be limited to service provision.

The second option, of tackling the root causes in the community of origin, was adopted by the organisation known as The Concerned for Working Children, in Bangalore, India. When the project first began to contact children working in catering establishments, garages, workshops, on the streets in a variety of jobs and as ragpickers, it discovered that a large number were migrants from rural areas.

This led to the development of a rural programme, which first looked for the reasons for migration. Village crafts were declining because plastic and synthetic articles were seen as more attractive and durable, and were marketed using aggressive techniques. So the project helped to organise groups of artisans to identify their problems and find solutions. This led to improved methods of production and design and better (collective) marketing of products. Children were taught these skills by older artisans.

At the same time, men, women and children were involved in meetings – as separate groups – for solving their own problems. The children asked for more information, so the wall newspaper *Bhima* was born. This is a monthly publication divided into two parts, a children's section in which children contribute their ideas in writing or pictures, and a 'learning' section that provides information on health, events and other children, making extensive use of cartoon strips. The children have formed their own association, Bhima Sangha, parallel to the adults' organisation, Nama Sabha.

The Undugu Society of Kenya is another programme that started with a curative approach, dealing directly with the parking boys of Nairobi, and then began to use preventative measures in the communities of origin, where they encourage people to take responsibility for their own lives. Over two decades it has expanded into community work, education schemes, income generation and national campaigning. Each stage of growth has entailed evaluation, rethinking and reorganisation.

Family reunification

When projects for street and working children are looking for alternatives to closed institutions such as orphanages, they naturally think about trying to reunite children with their own families. All other things being equal, this would always be the preferred choice. However, life has a way of being very unequal indeed and few projects have achieved much success with this option.

There is a very real sense in which project work aimed at reuniting street children with their parents is community work. It cannot be effective unless it is integrated with community and family development. Children who are simply sent home will often just as simply come back again to the streets. They may think they have just gone home for a visit. They may be unwelcome visitors, an extra mouth to feed or an irritant to a new step-parent. Unicef in Sudan once tried sending children home with a sack of food; this didn't work either.

Investigate family and child
The reason for some of the problems experienced in family reunification work is that it tends to focus on the child, rather than on the family. Yet, except in cases where natural disaster or conflict have separated families, the family is the reason why the child left home, whether it was a stay-away, run-away or throw-away situation. Thus there have to be changes on both sides for any reunion to be stable. This means resources for support, such as new skills in negotiating family relationships, better income, more space, opportunities in the community for the child.

FAMILY REUNIFICATION

We have to remember that it is not a reunification between ourselves and their families. It is their reunification, which implies a firm decision from both the families and the children. Such a decision will only be taken if the cause for the separation has been removed (Dallape, 1988, p41).

In general, family reunification schemes work on a case-by-case basis. Inevitably, this is child, rather than community, based so it fits somewhat uncomfortably with a development model. Nevertheless, family reunification should be regarded as community work, because children come from families that are part of communities. It is not just possible, but also essential, to ensure that family reunification work is carried out in a community context.

There are two main types of problem that have to be confronted in family reunification work, often at the same time. On the one hand, children may have come from abusive families, in which case family dynamics need to be addressed. On the other hand, they may be the product of impoverished families for whom reunification simply means the return of a burden they still cannot cope with. In either case, what is required is both preparation and follow-up

In many cases, families and communities will need to be informed about the lives the children have been living, for they may have imagined that everything was bound to go well in the city. Families also have to be willing to work at family dynamics. They may need to be provided with economic opportunities, so that they can afford to have the children at home and send them to school. In addition, local educational opportunities for children may need to be improved, provided, or made accessible. Ideally, the whole community should be involved in this process.

If family reunification is a chosen option, the project should establish with families what children will do when they get back home. Will they go to school, find work or help with family tasks? Much will depend on the opportunities available locally, so this entails work with the whole community, giving particular emphasis to its children.

Thus the child's desire to go home is not sufficient. You need to know how welcome he or she will be, within the family and within the community. Why did he leave? Was it because there was no future for him in the village, or because he could not get on with his stepfather? Why did she travel to the city? Was she running away from abuse or had she been recruited by a woman who said she would be a maid and go to school, but was really intending her for a brothel? Recruiters customarily give parents money, which is described as an advance on wages and may be vital for an impoverished family with younger children to feed. A child who has been sold in this way to pay off a debt or to raise credit can cause immense financial problems, even for parents who have been missing her and wishing to have her back home. If she has been working as a prostitute she may not be welcome. If families have believed their children were learning skills and getting a future in the town, there may be feelings of guilt or shame on both sides. When children return from the city, their new town habits may be disturbing influences on children and youth left behind.

Working with groups of families

One advantage is that children may often have come from the same rural area or the same slum. Thus it may be possible to work with groups of families. The YMCA in Bogotá works with families that have already lost one child to the streets, in order to prevent others following suit. Social workers not only counsel individual families, through a variety of participatory techniques, they have also organised families into self-help groups. This means that they not only work with family dynamics, but also try to address social and economic problems that families probably have in common.

Even when it can be organised on a group basis, family reunification is essentially a casework approach, which means it is demanding, labour intensive and expensive. Because of the cost, family reunification is likely to fall outside the scope of the majority of street and working children programmes (SCF Development Manual 3, *Family tracing: a good practice guide*, Bonnerjea, includes further discussion of the reunification process).

Children's organisations

A further community option is self-help groups with children. Both adult facilitators and older youth within the community can be used to help children organise themselves for their own benefit.

The example of Bhima Sangha, the children's group that runs parallel to an adult community organisation, in the project run by The Concerned for Working Children in Bangalore, has already been mentioned. Among many other activities, children from Bhima Sangha have, with adult help, carried out investigations into the deaths of working children, in hotel fires and fireworks factories, the findings of which they presented to the relevant authorities. This type of activity is a learning process in the widest and most significant sense, as the section of the report on the fireworks incident headed 'Sharing with Bhima Sangha Members' shows:

> We had to share our experiences with all our Bhima Sangha members who made the trip feasible. We related our experiences in a meeting called by the Bhima Sangha and discussed the journey, the hardships faced by the people of the area like the saline water, thorny bushes in our path, people we met, the disaster zone, responses of the labour officials and the Minister, the appeal we presented, etc. We also showed everybody the photos and we together listened to the taped sessions.
>
> The general reaction was, 'We should not abandon our efforts at this juncture. We should forward an appeal to the Chief Minister of Karnataka, signed by our friends in Bangalore and also send a letter to the President. We also felt that we should publish our findings in our wall magazine *Bhima* so that it could reach more of our friends.'

Children can also organise in such a way that they stimulate adult community work. This has been used as an approach to health education, most especially in the Child-to-Child approach (see further reading, p178). Children who learn about health care, food preparation, nutrition, hygiene in schools or health groups can successfully carry the message home and not only teach their families but also take responsibility for certain aspects of health in the home. Many health projects in Latin America during the 1992 cholera outbreaks used this approach and it could be argued that the prevention of a large-scale epidemic throughout the continent was achieved by its children.

One particularly successful child organisation is the movement of child and adolescent workers in Peru (MANTHOC), which now holds national and international meetings in which children share and debate the issues that are important to them. This movement was originally established by Catholic lay adults in 1977, and still has adult supervision. However, many of the adults now involved in MANTHOC are graduates of the movement, who were child leaders in their time. Although the movement began by organising child workers, it soon found itself involved in community work:

> Children working and living near a market in southern Lima were worried that rubbish which was discarded throughout the area was a serious health hazard. They organised a working party one day to burn the rubbish, but were dismayed to find that more was dumped there the following morning. It became clear that a regular municipal collection was the only way of solving the problem. To this end, the children organised a meeting locally and invited parents to join a campaign. Leaflets were delivered throughout the community and a petition signed and presented to the mayor, and eventually the local municipality agreed to provide a regular collection service (Boyden, 1988, p213).

ADVOCACY AND CAMPAIGNING

While service provision meets immediate needs and community work addresses long-term problems, advocacy and campaigning confront the root causes of the problems experienced by street and working children.

These options should not be confused with fundraising, although they frequently are, with negative effects for children. The emphasis throughout this manual has been on the strengths and capacities of children, rather than on their vulnerability. Much fundraising and many campaigns take the opposite approach, indulging in a pornography of misery, which may unloose some brief charitable responses, but fails to change attitudes and policies towards children.

The best kind of advocacy and campaigning involves children in defining their own problems and being helped to put their own case. It aims to inform and educate public and policy-makers and to bring about changes that will improve children's lives. The worst kind of advocacy and campaigning involves children in rallies and public shows arranged by adults who have decided what the issues are and parade children's misery in order to shock the public, to move them to pity and a generous donation to a project's funds.

Children should not be portrayed only as being helpless, vulnerable, exploited, starving and ill. Their words, pictures and stories should not be used without their permission. They should not be encouraged to tell their stories in public unless there is an expected positive outcome, with which they are in agreement.

USING THE WRONG IMAGES

A programme for street children depicted a poorly dressed, sad, destitute street urchin as part of their fundraising campaign. This appeals to the public's sensitivities and is very lucrative but it undermines the dignity of the street child witness to this portrayal and his respect towards the programme. It also serves to obscure the real issues regarding street children (Summing Up, 1990, p7).

Guidelines for advocacy and campaigning

Your project should include some element of advocacy and campaigning. This is best within the context of networking, and the ground rules are:

- Work within the framework of the Convention on the Rights of the Child, not just for street and working children but in the context of an improvement for all children.
- Be aware of and use country reports and alternative reports to the Committee on the Rights of the Child, where these exist.
- Work within the context of local law and justice.
- Use real, verifiable facts, never supposition, newspaper reports or hearsay.
- Remember that not all publicity is good publicity, especially for the children involved; emphasise the positive (what can be done) rather than the negative (degradation and vulnerability); make sure that children are not further stigmatised by publicity that marks them as criminals, drug addicts or prostitutes; it is far better to try to make a pact with those who are harming children in order to educate them and work together to improve the position than to denounce them as monsters, which will make them angry or defensive and might make the children's lives worse!
- Be sure that whatever activities you plan are aimed to bring about a practical or policy change that is agreed with the children involved; never ask children to do something you should do yourself, or that you wouldn't do yourself; remember that rallies, parades and demonstrations are attractive and photogenic, but also time-consuming and achieve very little.
- If your aim is to raise awareness remember that this needs follow-up Once people are interested, can you provide them with more information? Can

you use them as volunteers? What campaign should follow the raising of awareness? Campaigns are just like any other part of your project, they need to be planned. They must have objectives that relate to changes in attitudes, protection, provision and law.

* Don't bother to spend time and money on making a video – there are already far too many around.

CHILDREN ON PARADE IN MADURAI

More than a thousand children from neighbouring villages joined the participants of the workshop in demanding their rights. In order to bring the issue to public attention, a silent march was taken [through] the city.

The children carried a number of placards and posters, as well as a huge banner prepared during the workshop on which were painted various slogans: 'We want the elimination of child labour', 'Children are assets, not liabilities,' 'Right to childhood' and so on. Children and activists were also wearing T-shirts with similar messages across them; unfortunately, the children had no idea what was written on the T-shirt as it was in English. The purpose for which they had joined the activists on that day also seemed to be unknown to them ...

At various times during the workshop we had spoken of the child's need for a common platform and the children's right to be heard and involved in decision-making; what happened during the Public Action Day seemed to make a mockery of our discussions about children's participation (Caroline Wesley and Sreelata from The Concerned for Working Children, in *Molaké*, Vol 3, No 4, 1993, p28).

NETWORKING

At a meeting to share experiences of working with street children throughout Africa, held in 1990 in Zimbabwe, participants stressed one golden rule of project work that is all too seldom applied:

> The decision of which children the programme will focus on, and what service will be provided, should only be made on the basis of the programme's individual capacity. It was stressed that referrals between different programmes, catering for different types or groups of children, are important. **Not every organisation should try to deal with all children** (Summing Up, p8).

The typical situation for street children projects in particular is one of competition between agencies for funds, public attention and even for children. All the projects in any one city will claim to understand and solve the problem, and to use unique methods for achieving success. Obviously this cannot be the case and the competition results in duplication of efforts and wasted resources, neither of which benefits children. The best results have been achieved through cooperation between organisations and projects, so that resources, experiences and expertise are shared. Every project should have a unique and valuable contribution to make to a united effort and everyone has something to learn.

It may be that your local research has revealed just such a situation of confusion, suspicion and competitiveness. One project option is thus to initiate a network of agencies, which can include governmental, non-governmental and international organisations. Usually this will work best if there is a common objective, such as preparing an alternative report to the United Nations Committee on the Rights of the Child, campaigning on a specific issue or organising an awareness-raising event. The resulting group of agencies can then begin to form a more formal network, through which common aims can be pursued and resources shared. It should be clear which projects have the expertise to deal with particular groups of children, such as those with learning difficulties or drug users, or specific issues, such as counselling or vocational training. This provides a more integrated overall resource for children than they can possibly get in a situation where they may be forced to shop around from project to project, having their needs half met and playing off one set of service providers against another.

In India, city forums of projects for street and working children have been operating for some time with some success, not only in meeting the needs of children but also in raising the local profile of both working children and the projects themselves. The London-based Consortium for Street Children has even been able to raise funds jointly for member organisations.

It has been found that this type of cooperation works best if the network is serviced by a secretariat that can centralise organisation efficiently. It is possible for this function to be carried out by one of the larger, better-resourced organisations in a network, or by all members in rotation, but it is even better if funds can be raised for an independent secretariat, as is the case in Bombay.

EVALUATION

The chapter on research ended by looking at ways in which projects can develop systems to monitor their progress. This should be an integral part of project work, not just an annual review or an exercise carried out for or by donors, but part of day-to-day activities from which everyone can learn.

This process of continuous learning is part of both project and staff development and should take place at regular, specified intervals, which may be different for various levels of the project team. Thus in some projects staff members working directly with children may have a brief meeting at the beginning and end of each day, meet with their supervisors weekly, with a whole team meeting (including auxiliary workers) once a month and a management meeting with the board four times a year. Each of these meetings provides an opportunity to revisit objectives, consider success and failure, suggest new ways of approaching problems. Informal notes keeping a record of what is said are invaluable as a way of checking on progress. Every so often you need an 'away-day' to examine in depth any issues that may have arisen that require more time for consideration, away from the day-to-day pressures of the project – and just to remember why it was you started the work in the first place.

Fabio Dallape of Kenya's Undugu Society suggests that the project team needs to revise certain questions every three months. With respect to contact with children:

- What are the objectives of making contact? What are you trying to achieve – friendship? Confidence?
- How is this being achieved? Food? Clothes? Recreation? Business opportunities? Health?
- Why are particular methods being used?
- What are the advantages and disadvantages of these methods?
- What others might be used? Why are they not being used?
- Have the objectives of contacting children been achieved?
- Review the objectives – are they still the same? Do they need to be adapted?
- Are team members all clear about the objectives?

THE IMPORTANCE OF FLEXIBILITY

We have to be flexible ... capable of changing and adapting, because the societies in which street children live are constantly changing as a result of internal and external developments and we must, in turn, respond to these changes if we are to provide relevant assistance (Dallape, 1988, p11).

Continuous learning should produce records that will be helpful in collaboration with outside evaluators, who may be asked to make a report for an external funding body. Outside evaluation should not be regarded as a school examination where you 'pass' or 'fail' but a positive opportunity to learn using an outside resource.

As with using an external researcher, collaboration is the name of the game. Funding bodies (if involved), project staff and evaluator(s) should agree the terms of reference. The process of evaluation should be one in which staff are involved. The evaluation report should not be a secret document but shared with staff as part of project and staff development. These conditions should be established with the funding agency before contracts are signed and money received. (For more detailed discussion of monitoring and evaluation, see a forthcoming volume in the Save the Children development manual series, Gosling and Edwards, 1994.)

CHECKLIST OF QUESTIONS FOR PLANNING

- What is the target group (and why)?
- What has the project to offer this particular group in terms of expertise and resources?
- What are the problems of this group? Is this what the children say themselves? What solutions do they propose?
- What other projects are working with this group? Will your project be complementary to their work or in competition? How can you cooperate with other projects in the locality?
- What are the project objectives? Are these long-term or short-term?
- Are solutions temporary or permanent?
- What methods will you use to achieve your objectives?
- How will you measure success and failure?

Will the project be:
- A response to daily needs or an attempt to change the situation?
- Child or community focused?
- What will be the mix of service provision, development work and advocacy?
- Will the project be centre-based or outreach, or a mixture of both?

If you are providing services:
- Are these really needed by the children?
- Are other projects already providing these services?
- Can you provide these services adequately for the target group?
- Will children pay for services, and if so will this be a symbolic payment or cover costs?

If you are providing shelter:
- Will this be a shelter or a drop-in centre (or both)?
- Will it be a night shelter, or only operate in the daytime?

- Have you involved the neighbours in planning?

Above all:
- Take time to decide.
- Look at and learn from other projects.
- Involve the children in planning.

CHANGING AND BEING CHANGED

At first, though the volunteers tried hard to behave and act normally with them and tried hard to bridge the gap between them, they somehow betrayed the sense of being outsiders. They met the boys clinging on to their bags, lest they get stolen or become dirty. They wouldn't sit down comfortably lest their pants got dirty. And slowly the volunteers realised that this was in fact putting a distance between the boys and themselves. Then came the **conscious decision to do things like the street children and be like them**. They sat on the footpath, played with them, ate with them, experienced their occupations and even slept with them.

The street child's food is far from clean and he himself is forced to be farther from cleanliness. He sometimes doesn't take a bath for days. For fear of hospitals or a general apathy, his wounds ooze and a general atmosphere of filth is what he is compelled to live with. These live-in experiences with them brought home the realisation that a **process of delearning one's own myths and prejudices about street children is first required before beginning to 'contribute' to their lives**. That working with these children is by no means a one-way learning process but of mutual growth and development (YUVA, p4).

Chapter 6

ORGANISING HUMAN RESOURCES

This chapter considers what kind of structure the project will have, and what people will be involved in making it work.

CHILDREN

Children themselves are the best, the first, the most important resource. According to Undugu's experience of street children in Kenya (Dallape, 1988), they have the following potential:
- desire to learn, wish to have 'an education';
- knowledge of how to survive;
- experience of the difficulties of life and how to overcome or accommodate them;
- capability to organise themselves individually and in groups;
- solidarity and friendship in the group;
- solidarity with other poor;
- willingness to do any kind of job;
- creative in recreation.

This manual has frequently stressed the need to recognise children's strengths as well as their weaknesses. This is not always easy, because helping agencies are accustomed to treating children as helpless and vulnerable. Yet taking the first steps towards child participation can reap dividends. The Save the Children Jamaica project has found it very helpful to try to work more alongside children:

> We try to talk less and listen more. Give children a chance to come up with solutions. At times we use children to counsel other children, to look them up, etc. In these cases we find at times that both the counsellor child and the one being counselled benefits tremendously.

Making contact

As Fabio Dallape says, 'it is normal that street children don't trust us' (Dallape, 1988, p22). Their experience of most adults (including sometimes those who have said they want to help) is of rejection, beatings, condemnation. Their experience of do-gooders is that they offer silly things and are easily robbed or cheated.

Why should they want us to make contact?

Adults have power and have often used it badly over children. You cannot assume that street and working children want to meet you, or that you know about them. They already know too much about adults, you know little or nothing about them. You have to want to meet them, on equal terms. 'You must be prepared to meet them as they are, in their own environment, at their own time' (Dallape, 1988, p22).

In the case of street children it can be easy to make superficial contact because they are accustomed to being able to use adults in various ways, particularly to get money or other handouts. They know that most adults who are interested in them want to take photographs, hear sad life stories and be asked to take them home. This kind of contact is not useful for project work.

Don't waste time setting up meetings and calling them to attend. They won't come, or if they do, you won't listen to them.

Ways of making contact

One way of making contact, as both Fabio Dallape and Benno Glauser say, is to be out on the street playing with something. A simple toy such as a yo-yo will do. That will arouse children's curiosity, and an adult with a toy or game is less threatening, more attractive. Just hanging around with children over a period of time, joining in their games or quietly talking to them, without a camera or a notebook is the best way to make contact.

Once you have broken the ice, it is important to spend time with children, not asking questions but being with them and observing what they do. You don't need to take part in all the children's activities in order to be one of them – for example, you don't have to take drugs or steal in order to be 'accepted'. Although some street workers report that children require detailed explanations for not taking drugs, others state that children respect differences of this kind. There have even been some cases of street children trying to protect street workers from 'bad' street children who get drunk on alcohol or sniff glue.

YUVA staff report having negative experiences when they began working with street children. First they mapped an area of Bombay, with volunteers walking for hours at night, observing and identifying groups.

- One group, 'the elite of street children', was earning good money operating toy cars for gambling races on a 50/50 split with the owners. They had nowhere to keep their money, so spent it on gambling themselves. They worked late evenings and nights, so YUVA volunteers met them in the mornings, but the children were earning good money and had no incentive to join a project. In addition, the gambling bosses warned the volunteers off.

- YUVA also tried to work with a group of young drug addicts in one area. But they didn't care 'about the world and themselves'. They made threats against the volunteers. Then it was discovered that other NGOs were working in this area. So YUVA moved on again.

One way of making contact and working with the children was to go on the streets alongside them, which is what Altaf K Shaikh, a volunteer with YUVA, did. This is how he describes his experiences:

> To get a better insight into their lives and to try to establish a rapport with them, I decided to go ragpicking with them.
>
> I tried my best to look like them with a faded T-shirt, short pants and minus my chappals [sandals]. But, alas, my spectacles gave me away.
>
> Accompanied by three boys, I started at about 10am ... My friends got busy immediately, but it took me quite some time to adjust the gunny bag on my shoulder.
>
> At first I was self-conscious and hesitant, but soon, I stopped bothering. After getting soiled with a sticky bottle, I lost all my inhibitions. It did feel strange, though, to pick up bottle caps, plastic bags and other such trash that we are so used to throwing away at home ... (YUVA, p27)

Altaf made less money than the boys and had to be protected by them from a policeman that the children bribed. When he stayed overnight with the children some objected. This has been found also in other parts of the world. Street children have a right to privacy, like anybody else.

As already seen, the first step is the identification of need. Sometimes, as with water on Smokey Mountain or first aid on the streets of Bogotá, this is something an adult can do after observing the children and talking to them. Children can be clear about their wants in many ways. In 1980, the boys cleaning windscreens and selling newspapers at a crossroads in Kingston, Jamaica, were able to see the YMCA swimming pool through the railings from where they worked on the streets. It was a short step to ask them if they wanted to use it, and make it a condition to use the shower first. It is thus that a project can start.

But, as pointed out earlier, you need to make sure service and activities are relevant to the children and to strike a balance between what is free and what is paid for. Health care should normally be free, but children can feed and clothe themselves if they have money, and their independence is likely to be dear to them. If you help children to make better use of business opportunities this treats them as equals: a place to keep the bucket and rag of a car washer, to store goods for vending away from thieves, cooperative buying, a stand for car washing and other possibilities described in the last chapter.

What not to do

You should not:

- treat children with fear;
- under-estimate their intelligence;
- think of them as thieves;
- fail to understand their values;
- impose your own values, teaching, preaching, telling them things;
- imagine you know their values;
- imagine you know their needs and wants;
- be repelled by their appearance or habits, refuse to touch them, refuse to take food or drinks from them;
- compete with their times for work;
- create dependency by linking your visits to handouts;
- draw the attention of the public/police to them;
- think of yourself as noble;
- try to lure children into programmes with handouts or promises;
- make differences between groups of children that they do not make themselves;
- break up their existing networks and social groups.

What to do

You should:

- listen, and make sure you are really hearing;
- look, observe, record, reflect on what you see;
- learn, about them and about yourself.

STREETWORKERS MUST BE PATIENT

The 'outreach' worker should be someone whom the children can relate to and do not feel threatened by. The approach must be very informal and avoid intrusion. If a trusting relationship is to be formed, it is not advisable to meet a group of children with clip board, questionnaire and pen in hand. Little accurate information is shared with strangers on the streets, and patience is an essential element of the process (Summing Up, p8).

Child participation

In an ideal situation children should participate at all levels of project planning, operation and evaluation. They should be part of each process from the beginning.

However, this is the goal, and as such will not be totally possible in the early planning stages. After all, it is adults who first saw the children working or on the street and decided to do something about it.

Nevertheless, planning to involve children *is* part of the early stages. This involvement should be thought of as:
- sharing power between adults and children;
- adults and children treating each other as equals.

Learning to participate

To begin with, neither the adults nor the children will have the skills to do this. It is a learning process for both parties:

> Participation is where the responsibility and control of the process of development are in the hands of those who are intended to benefit from the process. How do we achieve real participation? **Through transferring the skills of analysis, action, design and planning** (Dallape & Gilbert, 1993, p15).

In order to be able to make decisions about project plans and project work, children usually have to acquire new skills. They need to be able to think about their experiences and analyse them, to find out about the options available and be able to make decisions about what choices to take, based on being able to think through what the consequences may be. Then they need to be able to evaluate the results of their decisions over time, so that they can make further choices.

In order to be able to help children learn these skills, adults also have to acquire new skills. These are new ways of listening, based on rethinking their relationship to all children. The way adults normally behave towards children is that they:
- deny children's perceptions ('But you know you don't really like to be on the streets');
- assert the superiority of adult opinion and will ('I've come to help you because I don't like to see you sleeping on the streets');
- repress children and emphasise adult ability to use force ('If you don't come and stay in the project the police will take you to prison').

Learning together

Working with children, rather than for them, means focusing on ways in which adults and children discover and learn together. Children should be involved in project management as soon as possible, increasing their participation from the research stage onwards as a gradual move towards sharing power. They should be consulted at every stage, but this does not mean making the mistake of thinking that their word is somehow sacred. In the literature on child participation there is a good deal written about the importance of 'the children's voice', as if children have some kind of special insight. These books tend to be written by romantic Westerners, who are thinking of childhood as a time of special truth. Even though they claim to be part of a new way of thinking about children, they have not really broken away from the image of children as innocent and close to nature. One wonders what they would do when confronted with the following scenario:

- The street children shelter is new and the workers are committed to child participation, holding daily meetings with the residents to take decisions about activities and rules. One morning project workers find that a boy has run amok during the night, wrecked all the new tables and chairs and painted obscenities on the walls. They call the culprit before the whole group of children and ask what punishment he should suffer. The children pass the death sentence.

Clearly, workers need to guide children through a number of progressive decision-making situations, including explaining why they make certain choices themselves and being open to criticism. Children's voices can be heard in all project planning and management meetings. But they do not necessarily have priority, although there will be situations in which they do. Project management should be constantly seeking more and better ways in which children can participate, discussing this with children, making innovations and evaluating the effects. The ladder of participation drawn by Roger Hart, which is on page 34, provides a simple way of making regular checks on the way the project, and individual adults within it, are bringing about increasing child participation.

It is important that this process is one of mutual learning rather than one in which adults patronise children and decide when they are 'ready' to take decisions or responsibilities. Street and working children have already borne a good deal of responsibility in their lives, and this should be channelled creatively.

STAFF

Street educators

There is some mystique attached to staff working on projects dealing with street and working children. Much of this is associated with what are called 'street educators', a term associated with the Latin American, non-institutional model of street children project. Street educators contact children on the streets and encourage them to be involved in project work. In reality, their role is more one of contacting and befriending, often including health services and counselling, than educating.

It is sometimes assumed that street educators must be male, and tough males at that. But this is far from true.

- Many successful street educators are female; it can be harder for street children to show aggression to women than to men.
- Although the vast majority of children living on the streets are boys, many girls work on the streets.
- Even the toughest street boys need opportunities to make friendships with women.

Many projects have found it productive for street educators and other street workers to operate in pairs, one man and one woman. This can be less threatening for both the children and the workers. Children can, in fact, be very protective; during a period of community violence in Colombo a female member of Redd Barna staff was afraid to leave the project: 'Some of the older boys demanded that she took off her gold earrings and bracelets. Then they took care of her purse and escorted her home through a labyrinth of safe side streets' (What's Inside?, p35). Of course, it can be difficult for women street educators. Diana Vasquez, who used to work at the SCF San Pedro Sula project, wrote in a report that 'It was very difficult for the children to accept a female street educator, because it was the first time that a woman had approached them with the intention of making friends'. The worst problem for Diana, however, was the police. On three occasions she was arrested. But this happens to male street educators also. The public too can be aggressive towards outsiders they see talking to street children.

Recruitment

THE IMPORTANCE OF BEING PROFESSIONAL

... the children have the right to deal with motivated and trained staff. We should be critical about the quality of our staff. Too often we have an attitude of 'anything is better than nothing, implying that whatever we offer to street children is good. Do we offer our children as a teacher, the first person we meet on the street? It is not enough that such a person is generous and loves children. Let us offer them people who are professionally prepared to deal with the proposed subjects (Dallape, 1988, p33).

Staff for work with street and working children do not come freshly trained with that label on them. Recruitment is a matter of judging potential rather than looking at qualifications, although training in psychology, social work and teaching have all proved useful. It is not enough to have a good heart and intentions. Practical experience of working in interactive ways with children is important and it is often helpful to recruit from the community. It is worth remembering that project staff need to be able to relate to the community as a whole, and not just to children.

In some cases, street educators are older youth who have graduated from a project. Sometimes it is claimed that only people who have been on the streets themselves can understand or communicate with street children. Activists taking this approach often sneer at professional qualifications and claim that only people with special empathy can work with children who have experienced particular difficulties in their lives. There are a number of reasons why this approach should be challenged:

- Because it treats street and working children as if they are a different kind of human being.
- Because, although the authenticity of people who are ex-street children or ex-prostitutes cannot be challenged, it may not be helpful. To define yourself as an ex-street child is not a whole or healthy identity. To be genuinely helpful to children you need to be an ex-ex-street child, to be able to distance yourself from your own problems and not confuse them with the children's problems.
- Because the distinction between those who have the special knowledge derived from having been on the streets and those who do not can create a split within a project team.
- Because people who work on an empathetic or emotional level, however 'good with children' they may seem to be, usually refuse to be accountable. They cannot explain their methods and have a personalised way of working that can be neither replicated by other workers nor monitored.
- Because there is no mystery about working with any children in especially difficult circumstances. There are established methods and models, as in the SCF development manual *Communicating with children: helping children in distress.*

Management methods and structures

After finding the best possible human resources it is important that they should be organised, trained and supported.

Cooperation and group management

A cooperative, group management approach is better than an authoritarian structure. Staff in all parts of the project should be aware of and respect each other's roles. If you are working in a stressful situation, teamwork and mutual dependence are important. One of the first decisions to be made with respect to staffing is the extent to which workers will have specialist roles or take on a mixed workload. Because continuity is important when working with any children, and particularly for children who need to be able to develop stable relationships with the project, it is important to 'double up' staff so that activities and relationships are neither interrupted nor ended when a particular staff member becomes ill or leaves.

Most people are more accustomed to rigid management styles than to flexible group management. They feel more comfortable if the director sits behind a desk, workers are ranked in order of importance and responsibility and the cook and watchman, at the bottom of the scale, do not take part in management debates. But this kind of structure is impossible to use if the aim is to encourage child participation. Children will be quick to spot the hypocrisy of being told they are equal with adults if adults do not treat each other as equals.

THE NEED FOR STAFF SUPPORT

There is little doubt that at an individual level, sustained contact with some street children reveals significant psychopathology, ranging from more neurologically based attention-deficit disorders to a predisposition for developing serious personality disorders. Staff members will need help to recognise, understand and deal with such psychological problems. Some youths will tend to rely on immature defences such as projection, acting out, passive-aggression which is especially tough for staff members to work with. Thus, professional advice, finding concrete ways to help staff deal with these behaviours, can prove useful. It is important to allocate resources for assessment diagnosis and planning of treatment of the disturbed children (Summing Up, p25).

Group management requires high levels of support, team building and supervision. This can be achieved through regular meetings, encouraging supportive relationships and also seeking supervision for staff from outside bodies. In pressurised work, where staff deal with difficult emotions, demands and challenges every day, it is important to be able to discuss problems experienced with particular children, feelings of inadequacy, anger or failure. Part of developing supportive relationships within the project comes from setting up opportunities for these issues to be aired, in team meetings and in one-to-one sessions as and when needed. It is also ideal if a semi-formal supervision arrangement can be established with an outside agency. This could be achieved through exchange with another NGO, or an arrangement with a school of social work or a social services agency.

It may not be costly. An academic social work department might be grateful for the opportunity to exchange the services of their staff as supervisors for placement opportunities for their students.

Similar expert help can often be organised from other professional groups, to supplement staff skills in particularly difficult cases. Educationalists, psychologists and social workers can help project workers to recognise when children have particular problems and to support the project in coping.

There is a downside to group management. It means work for everyone and sometimes makes it hard to take tough decisions. This is well illustrated by Nandana Reddy's description of a particular problem in the project The Concerned for Working Children.

> A very embarrassing, tricky, uncomfortable and displeasing aspect of NGO work involves being forced to take disciplinary action against one's colleagues. It is a very delicate situation: you are preaching justice, equality and human rights, but when it comes to your own staff you don't know how to deal with it ... You are not sure that you can be fair and firm at the same time – most of us do not know how to deal with such situations.
>
> We were faced with a situation of this kind last year. Seven of our field activists [street educators] were found to be negligent. They were just not working but refused to admit this ... Our Executive Committee advised disciplinary action but we could not bring ourselves to initiate proceedings. We felt uncomfortable and treacherous – betrayers of the cause ...
>
> We let things drag on for an interminable eight months, all the while keeping channels of communication open in the hope that a settlement would be reached. We finally succeeded and received their resignations in return for a cash payment (in *Molaké*, Vol 3, No 3, 1993, p7).

The project remained uneasy with this solution. Perhaps this could be seen as a precedent that other negligent workers could use to their advantage. It was decided to keep better records in order to be able to produce proof when necessary. It was also decided to work collectively to establish a set of 'framing rules' that listed rights and responsibilities of all workers.

Collective standards of behaviour

Standards of behaviour should also be set collectively. These include avoiding the development of highly personal relationships between a child and a particular adult, and children calling staff mummy and daddy. There is a balance to be developed and maintained. Staff cannot and should not enter into long-term parent-like relationships with children, but the children do crave affection and emotional response, and this must be met. Staff do not need to be particularly tough, but they should be quietly confident in their own emotional strengths. They should not need the children's affection, or be too eager to be liked. Male staff should be discouraged from acting out tough male roles with boys in the project.

Another issue may be staff dress, particularly when workers come from a different economic or social group from the community in which the project works. For example, mothers of children in the Redd Barna project in Sri Lanka at first did not want to join in activities because they felt uncomfortable with the western clothes worn by staff, which failed to cover legs and arms adequately. Staff should also be discouraged from wearing old or dirty clothes at work. How can children gain pride in themselves if you demonstrate so clearly what you think of them? They are less likely to be envious of you for having better clothes than to be pleased to be seen with someone well-dressed.

Issues such as these should be subject to constant review at team meetings. Otherwise it is too easy for front line workers to develop stereotyped responses to children, police and public. The children become clients, the police the enemy, the public stupid. Then workers are threatened with burn out, the children are no longer treated with respect as individuals, and stimulating, innovative work simply doesn't happen.

Children's complaints about staff
These are the complaints street children in Manila had about project staff:
'We do not like STAFF
- who manhandle us, who mete out too hard punishment, especially physical punishment
- who demand heavy work from us: eg, digging wells or [latrines]
- who demand that children feel indebted to them for the services rendered
- who are not loving or affectionate enough
- who give attention only when we do something wrong
- who do not appreciate what we can do
- who play favourites
- who pretend to be caring when there are visitors, but are not truly caring
- who ask us a lot of questions without explanation
- who fight among themselves in front of us children
- who swear and curse
- who are always speaking English
- who stay in their offices and do not relate with us children
- who spend the whole day talking nonsense
- who are gullible
- who demand that schedules be religiously followed, but they themselves do not always follow the schedule' (Street children in Asia, pp18-19).

Training

As Matthew Thomas, of the Khar Danda project in Bombay, has been heard to say, street education is a vocation and not a job. A master's course in social work is of little use if the individual is uncomfortable on the streets, and it is experience rather than training courses that makes street educators.

But vocation is also not enough. The work needs discipline, training and evaluation. A street educator who will not be accountable for his or her work with children is irresponsible at best, and at worst may be a child abuser. Projects must be clear about this and insist on professional behaviour.

However good with children a person is when they start the job they can still improve, reflect on what works and does not work, and share this experience with others. Street education must be systematised, and must be replicable. If it is all inspiration you cannot tell if it is helpful or harmful for the children. These children are already damaged by society, to run the risk of further, inexcusable, harm is immoral.

The need for training street educators, however able, is best understood in comparison with ballet dancers: the talent may be innate and the will to dance strong, but the perfection of the prima ballerina is only achieved through years of hard work, discipline and training.

THE IMPORTANCE OF HUMAN RESOURCES

Staff development is the major issue in the general development of such a project. What the staff cannot do, cannot be done. There are few material inputs required. The project will stand or fall according to the development of its human resources (What's Inside?, p17).

There are few training courses for street workers available and they are unlikely to operate in your area. Some contacts and materials derived from well-established projects are listed later in this manual. Otherwise, you need to be cautious about some of the training on offer. Some projects, for which there is no evaluation available, have declared themselves successful after a brief period of operation and set themselves up as trainers. If your staff attend these courses they will only learn about one (unproven) method.

It may be more important for staff to upgrade their skills in various areas that supplement the less clear-cut skills of street education. For instance, all staff need to be trained in basic first aid, including office staff, cooks and drivers. All staff are part of the team and need staff development. Given that street workers come in all shapes and sizes, it is worth carrying out a skills audit to see what resources you can count on and what is missing. It may be the case that one street educator is a skilled needlewoman, for example, and could run a sewing class if that is what children require. The driver may also be able to teach basic car repair. But all staff may lack information about topics such as primary health care, HIV or nutrition for which training may be available locally.

Lessons are learned daily in all projects, but this learning is seldom shared, systematised or recorded. In-house staff development and training should take place continuously through regular meetings to incorporate staff observations and feedback. Regular reflective meetings of this kind make it possible for the work of the project to move 'from an impressionistic muddle to a reasonably structured programme which can be sustained over some time' (What's Inside?, p17).

VOLUNTEERS

Volunteer staff

In many projects, particularly in the early days, staff are all unpaid volunteers. The comments about staff apply to volunteers, who should be made to feel part of the team. It is helpful for volunteers if their specific roles and responsibilities are agreed before they begin working with the project and if they have a particular task given to them. Goodwill can evaporate if no one seems to know what the volunteer should be doing and he or she is just sent off to do a different menial task on each visit. Volunteers should be respected for the time they are giving to the project, not undervalued because their labour is free. Time is money and they are giving their time.

Although using voluntary help may seem to be a good way of increasing human resources, the organisation and management of volunteers may actually prove to be more trouble than it is worth in a small project. Management of volunteers takes staff time and can be just one extra burden for over-stretched staff.

Volunteers on management boards

Every project should have a board of management that takes overall responsibility for the proper running of the project. The people who serve on the board are a special kind of volunteer not only giving up their time but also making a long-term commitment to the project. Boards of management need to be regularly informed about the project's plans and progress, which can often mean

considerable education about the children and the best ways of working with them. A supportive, well-informed board of management will:
- act as a buffer against outside forces that might threaten the project;
- provide additional resources, or act as a channel to other resources;
- help to raise funds through contacts, skills or adding credibility.

Choosing the correct board members is important. It is all very well to get a cluster of important names, but will they have the time and commitment to come to meetings regularly or give up their time in other ways?

Board members can provide strategic links with other groups in society. Thus it can be useful for the security of the project or the safety of the children to have a member of the police or judiciary on the board, or at least an active lawyer. Representation from the world of commerce can unlock funds and resources. Someone from the medical profession provides both expertise and contacts with hospitals and clinics, just as a member from the educational sphere can make links with teachers and schools.

In addition, a project that aims to use participatory methods also needs representatives of the staff, the community within which it works and, most importantly, the children themselves.

LOCAL GOVERNMENT

There is a sense in which projects for street and working children always find themselves on the edges of the law. Street children are outside society and child work is illegal. NGOs working with these groups perform an important task for government by dealing creatively with a problem that might otherwise require the force of the law, taking children into orphanages or remand homes. This means that the NGO effort can always be disowned by the authorities if things go wrong and praised if things go well according to the official view of things. It is for this reason that links with local administration and the legal profession through the board of management are advisable.

It is important not to treat government agencies as enemies but to try to work alongside them and complement their efforts. Thus the supplementary work of non-formal education can be of great value to the formal school system, and experiences or resources can be exchanged. This may provide an opportunity for educating officials about the conditions of children's lives and for making an input to changing policies.

INSTITUTIONS

Religious bodies

Many street children projects are run by Christian organisations, which have a preference for orphanages even though some orders, such as the Salesians, have been particularly active in promoting alternative, non-institutional approaches.

From the point of view of organising resources for your project you will probably find that a Christian group is among the NGOs that is working with the target group of children locally and will be among the agencies with whom you should be networking.

Local religious institutions can be a source of both funds and other resources. Most religions carry an obligation to be charitable and Islam, for example, entails a particular responsibility for children. The buildings associated with places of worship such as mosques and churches may open their doors and facilities to projects, providing space, food and clothing (although religious bodies too need educating about the disadvantages of handouts).

Although these may seem to be the most accessible resources, in some places they have proved otherwise, finding all manner of reasons to refuse, such as the delinquency of street children.

Voluntary bodies

The importance of networking and cooperation between NGOs in the field of street and working children has already been emphasised. But NGOs that do not have a special interest in this group may still provide valuable resources. Youth clubs and YMCAs may lend recreation facilities, as well as supplying volunteers. Scouts and guides have also provided support for children's projects. All these institutions have proved particularly useful in organising residential camps for disadvantaged children. Both club members and the children from projects benefit from learning about each other's lives and experiences.

Schools

As education is the major formal institution for children, links with schools are vital for projects, particularly if they aim to provide children with access to formal education. School buildings are potential out-of-hours facilities for non-formal education activities, in which not only children from the project but also children who are falling behind at school can take part.

Health facilities

Access to health care is a perennial problem for street and working children. Links with hospitals, clinics, doctors, nurses and dispensaries can provide:
- opportunities for emergency treatment when necessary;
- training possibilities for staff;
- educational opportunities for children, including visits to hospitals;
- volunteers for the project;
- a source of medical supplies and advice.

COMMUNITIES AND FAMILIES

Community involvement begins with contacts with local leaders, who may be part of local administration, political parties, grassroots organisations, women's groups or traditional leaders, such as chiefs in African countries or village panchayats in India.

The community involved may be the one in which the project is located, the place where the children live now or in the area from which they have migrated.

THE CHILDREN DO LIVE IN COMMUNITIES, BUT DO THE COMMUNITIES KNOW THEM?

Street children associate themselves with certain geographical areas where they perceive resources to be available for their survival. A place to sleep undisturbed, a place to wash clothes, a place to take a bath, a place to look for food, be it only in the garbage cans, a place to provide services in exchange for some money, a place to make friends. These places are located in communities and community members can play an important role in helping street children to survive with dignity and, with external support, enabling street children to develop (Dallape, 1988, p34).

Undugu reports that chiefs and local leaders could be involved when children found in urban areas had migrated from the same rural area. In 1981, the authority of chiefs helped to get a particular group of boys back to their home village, in schools with uniforms. Traditional and popular leadership both help to integrate project work into communities.

A further specific source of support for the project and the children within the community are parents' groups, which may be either parents from the community in general, or parents of street and working children who can form support groups. Parents' groups can serve a number of purposes:

- Education and awareness-raising about the welfare of children and children's rights within the family and the community.
- Mutual support between families.
- Fundraising to support children who are returning to school, through providing books and uniforms.
- Setting community standards for child welfare and acting as a watchdog to ensure that these are met, particularly with respect to violence against children and other forms of abuse.

You should try to ensure that 'parents' include fathers (and stepfathers). All too frequently a parents' group consists entirely of women.

COMMERCE

Social associations of business people, such as the Rotary Club, the Lions and the Soroptimists, both local and international, have a long history of supporting projects for disadvantaged children with funds and gifts in kind. The local association can also unlock the door to the business community for other types of support.

Nevertheless, it seems to be easier to motivate the small business community to help children. Stallholders in markets, small shop and restaurant owners, although often far from wealthy themselves, often help street and working children spontaneously by offering food, shelter, employment opportunities, emotional support and friendship These individuals can become powerful community allies and additional resources for any project. The Undugu informal sector training programme relies on the services of artisans in the slums who offered to train young people. By 1988, over 80 craftsmen were involved in training a total of 180 young people – some of whom were very volatile – and preparing them for government tests.

The wider business community, more distant from the day-to-day problems of marginalised children, usually needs publicity and education before being motivated to give practical help Once they are involved, their commercial expertise can provide innovative project options.

- The company involved in Project Hot Pot in Bombay has vending machines for drinks in various large companies. Street children serve workers with drinks from the machines and are paid from the profits (of course, this would only function in a place where it is not customary for workers to go and serve themselves from drinks machines).

- Also in Bombay, a 'teenage academy' has been established for vocational training, with an agreement with two local companies that they will employ a number of street children.
- Again in Bombay, some companies have sponsored street children to clean the beaches where they sleep, so that the children are seen as a positive rather than a negative presence.

All these activities have arisen in the context of the Bombay forum for street children organisations, underlining the importance of networking and cooperation.

POLICE

Although, strictly speaking, the police are an element of local government, their presence on the streets is so important for street children that they are here treated as a separate issue.

Police forces are the agents of government and society that have the most consistent relationship with street and working children. They are empowered to clear children off the streets, stop illegal street trading, arrest drug users, beggars, prostitutes and thieves. They are also empowered to seek runaway children, rescue abused children and those who are employed in illegal and exploitative work, including arresting employers in some cases.

It is not surprising therefore that Jo Boyden says, 'the police are part of the problem, they are also part of the solution' (in Black, 1993). They can be harnessed to support the project. But they need information and education. All they know about street children is that they infringe the law in a number of ways, and they offend respectable citizens. Police are empowered to clean the streets. They need another perspective.

Police harassment and violence

As it is, most street children everywhere will tell you that their main problem is police harassment, even violence. The Street Wise project in South Africa describes a typical situation: 'The police are tough on street children. In Durban, two boys who joined a gang of petty thieves were shot in the back and killed when they were scaling the wall of a residential property. In Johannesburg, Street Wise have had boys arrested by the police, who have never been seen again' (Summing Up, p19).

The deaths of street children in some Latin American countries at the hands of police and other bodies have been widely publicised recently in the western press, often quite cynically to raise funds for organisations and programmes that have little to do with street children and could not affect the violence shown to them. What this publicity both reveals and conceals is an underlying situation in most countries where street children are found, in which they are subjected to verbal, physical and often sexual abuse at the hands of police and others on the streets, in police cells, remand homes, prisons and detention centres.

Curiously, it is often in those countries where the worst police abuse is to be found that police authorities may be most progressive, developing plans to counteract violence together with policies that include employing social workers and police, many of whom are women, with special responsibility for children. It is important, therefore, to make a distinction between different levels of police and policing when you first research your local area. Violence towards children on the streets is carried out by local police, who have had little in the way of education and training, encouraged implicitly or explicitly by certain sections of the local public. The special forces set up to protect children frequently translate into squads of police cars that tour the city centre at night to pick up children and place them in a government project, often a closed institution. This is just a more sophisticated version of cleaning the streets.

Education can make a difference. In Maharastra Police Academy a training programme about street children is now an annual feature for 500 trainees. The course uses resource people from the street children forum in Bombay, although Joseph Junior, the Director, says the curriculum could do with more input from academic institutions. Teenage street children have also been resource people, using drama to introduce the problems as they saw them. The course does not rely on formal teaching methods alone, but also uses video and lectures, group discussions and ice-breaking games, all unfamiliar techniques to police accustomed to rigid teaching discipline. At first, says Joseph, 'they found this quite ridiculous', but from the second day onwards there was an attitude change.

Cooperation with police

This education led to an interesting cooperation with the traffic police in Bombay, which was suggested by the police themselves. At peak times, pedestrian traffic in this vast overcrowded metropolis reaches extraordinary levels. The pavements become dangerously congested and the passage of people on foot threatens to block the already dense road traffic. Older children have been trained to help constables control pedestrian traffic at peak times of day. They have six days training, in leadership camps, over a six-month period. Because of the requirements of child labour law, the 21 children involved are all aged 15 years or more. The children have a uniform that they care for themselves, sponsored by a motor company and bearing its logo alongside that of the forum for street children. After the first year of operation the police were so pleased with the success of the project that they decided to train 16 more children.

When children are reunited with families in rural areas, the local police may be the first contact with parents in the village, so they may need to be encouraged to take on the role of counsellor. Thus police should be harnessed alongside community leaders. They can be powerful allies but, if they do not have information, they can be a negative force, stigmatising as thieves and runaways the children who have returned from the city.

Some projects in urban areas have cooperated with police to develop various schemes. One technique that has been tried in several places is for children who attend a street children project to carry identity cards that protect them from police harassment. Reports of these schemes vary and there are no outside evaluations available through which they can be judged. It seems that police do not always understand the purpose of the cards, and use them as an excuse for further abuse. The schemes may be of limited scope, relating only to one project. Thus children who are not in that project, or not in any project at all, suffer from a disadvantage. Then, of course, cards can be lost or stolen. And children do not always like to be identified as street children.

Identity cards illustrate that a project that is regarded as legitimate can provide certain kinds of security for children. It is worth cooperating with authorities at the very least to try to ensure that a drop-in centre or night shelter is a 'no-go' area for police, that will not be raided in a search for thieves or drugs. Even church premises are not immune from such police invasions, which can make children very wary of going there again.

Many projects have taken this place of safety idea further and established, not just with the police but also with the courts, that they can provide an alternative to remand homes and prisons for children who break the law. David Tolfree writes in a report for SCF that, in 'Child Workers in Nepal' (CWIN), 'staff are beginning to secure more formal police cooperation in some aspects of their work. They are now seeking the early release of young people from prison, on the basis that personal support and income generation activities will be provided, and that young people will be returned to prison to serve their sentences if they do not conform to the requirements of CWIN staff.' In Tijuana, on the border between Mexico and the United States, staff of a YMCA street children project have negotiated a desk alongside immigration officers, where they help to assess children who are returned to Mexico after illegally crossing the border alone. In most cases children are released into the project's care rather than being sent to prison, which would be the only other official response.

If a project has this kind of credibility with the police and legal authorities, it can be a power for justice for individual children who are accused of breaking the law, speaking in court on behalf of children who would otherwise have no voice raised in their defence, bailing children out of unsuitable remand or prison accommodation where they mix with adult prisoners, and using these experiences in general advocacy for the rights of children to fair treatment before the law.

Projects for working children may be able to work alongside police, locating particularly abusive employers and ensuring that they are brought to justice. Children who are rescued from these situations need special care, rehabilitation and often, to be reunited with their families. Cooperation with police can ensure that they are cared for by the project rather than being immediately removed to an orphanage that cannot cater for their special needs, or released to the dubious safety of the streets and slums with no alternative work or accommodation provided.

Nevertheless, in all these examples of successful cooperation it should not be forgotten that 'the police are part of the problem'. It may not always be feasible or desirable to cooperate with police, particularly in those countries where the force is especially corrupt or particularly violent towards street children. One disadvantage of such cooperation is that the project may be identified with the police and raise the suspicions of children. Police may demand, or seize, individual files kept on children. They can use the relationship with the project to gain, or fabricate, information that could be used to close it down.

The bottom line is that projects need to act with discretion in their relationship with police. They should neither indulge in fierce condemnation, making accusations that cannot be backed up with factual evidence or that will not stand up in court, nor imagine that their cooperation with the police makes them immune from any kind of investigation. As a safeguard, it is always helpful to work closely with sympathetic and accredited human rights lawyers, who can both advise on the suitability of evidence and help build a defence case if necessary.

QUESTIONS TO ASK YOURSELF

- To what extent are children involved in the planning, running and evaluation of the project?
- Do you have a structured plan for children's participation to increase over time?
- What kind of staff structure does the project have?
- Have you carried out a resource audit of staff skills?

- Does this include all workers?
- How can existing staff skills be used to improve the project?
- Do you have a plan for staff development and training?
- What opportunities are provided for workers to share their experiences and build on what they have learned from children?
- How is the project's learning process being recorded?
- Can you describe project work in a systematic fashion, so that it could be understood and replicated by another project?
- What opportunities are provided for workers to be supported through difficult work experiences?
- What are the agreed standards of worker behaviour?
- Do you have a written and agreed list of tasks and responsibilities for each worker?
- What is the agreed disciplinary procedure?
- Do you have a plan for working with volunteers?
- Are volunteers included in the resource audit and training schemes?
- What are the resources available to you from:
  - the board
  - local schools
  - local health facilities
  - voluntary bodies
  - religious institutions
  - local government
  - commerce
  - communities
  - parents?
- Are you using these resources to the full? If not, why not? What would be the best way of unlocking this potential? Who on your board or project team has the best contact?
- What is your relationship with the police?
- What could or should it be?
- How can you build on the project's standing with the police and the courts so that the children's security is improved?
- Do you have firm contact with lawyers who can support you and your work?

Chapter 7

COMMON PROBLEMS, SUGGESTED SOLUTIONS

Every project has its own history and its own problems, but some difficulties have cropped up time and time again. Some of the most common difficulties encountered by projects, particularly those working with street children, are discussed in this final chapter.

EMOTIONAL DEPENDENCY

Where there is a close association between a worker's personality and the project, children, parents and communities can see themselves as relating to an individual rather than to a project or agency. This personal relationship can be meaningful for a child, particularly for the most disruptive or difficult children who may only relate to the project occasionally through a particular worker to whom they run in times of trouble. Discussing a girl who had caused endless problems running away from her family and the project, but still coming back to see her, Glenda Drummond of Save the Children Jamaica commented, 'If the child reaches you, you have reached her.'

There is obviously some meaning and strength in the relationship for such a child, which may show good results later in life despite present failure. But the negative effects of a close personal relationship can be burn out for the worker and dependency for the child.

Dependency can also occur the other way around. Project workers can be emotionally dependent on children. This can take three forms:

- Because children do not have power in society, working with them is attractive to some adults who are uncertain about their own status among other adults. They may need to work with children because this makes them feel powerful. This power can be misused through physical punishment or simply ordering children around. Adults like this will not attract children to a project, nor will they encourage true child participation. But they may pass off the way they interact with children as being necessary because the children lack discipline.

- Because children whose lives have been difficult may crave affection and cling to any adult who pays them attention, working with them is satisfying to adults who need to feel needed. They may encourage close personal relationships with individual boys or girls, who call them 'Mummy' or 'Daddy'. If the child begins to believe this it can be devastating when a pretend parent leaves the project for work elsewhere, giving the child yet another experience of abandonment. Meanwhile, other children may resent project workers having 'favourites' and the worker's judgement is clouded by his or her 'love' for a particular child.

THE NEED FOR LOVE AND ATTENTION

It is a difficult target group to contact since they are in need of love and attention more than any other group They touch you and want to be touched ... Almost immediately, they express the desire to come and live with you. They need a father. They need a mother, they need a friend (Dallape, 1988, p29).

- Because many children in projects are attractive, crave love and lack power, working with them is attractive to adults whose emotional lives are unsatisfactory. As in all work that brings adults into close personal relationships with children, there is a danger that emotional dependency and physical contact may lead to sexual abuse. This is particularly likely (and particularly unforgivable) with street children who may already be sexually active before they come into contact with the project. Sexual relationships may be the only way they know of getting attention, favours and cuddles from adults. They have no one to turn to for help except project workers. Other adults often fail to recognise that sexual abuse is taking place, preferring instead to idolise adults who work with street children, who are doing a job the rest of society wants to forget about. This is an unforgivable betrayal of children.

The best way to counteract these problems is right at the start when you recruit staff. It is as important to probe why people want to work with children as to look at paper qualifications. In addition, it is wise to institute the following practices in projects:

- In the course of everyday work with children, project workers should routinely work in pairs, so that continuity of contact with children is maintained even when a worker leaves.
- Children should be gently discouraged from calling workers 'Mummy' and 'Daddy'.

- Relationships between adults and children in the project should be one of the regular topics of discussion in team meetings and standards of behaviour agreed.

Because we are all human beings there are bound to be children who are special for each one of us; and that is healthy and important for the children. But there is a fine line between this and unhealthy, dependent or abusive behaviour. Teamwork means developing open relationships, so that workers' needs for affection and emotional support can be met. This is one of the reasons why outside supervision of the project was suggested in the last chapter.

'DISRUPTIVE' CHILDREN

What can you do about a child who constantly fights with other children, brings knives or other weapons on to the premises, attacks project workers, steals, shouts and is abusive?

It is easy to say, 'He is acting out his feelings of aggression', or 'She needs attention'. Psychological theories do not help much when you have stopped the ninth fight of the day, equipment is broken, programme work has not progressed and smaller children are crying. Then you may be faced with the difficult choice between meeting the needs of one particularly damaged child, and the safety and development of many others in the project.

What can you do? If you throw the 'disruptive' child out, is this a permanent exile, or just to teach her a lesson? Will you take her back when she begs to return and says she has changed? How do you judge if he has really changed? What do you do when he begins to fight or take drugs all over again? Can you afford to put the whole project at risk for one violent child? What about the personal safety of staff and other children? What if his behaviour attracts unwelcome police attention to the project?

Children who act out their problems by disrupting activities, or who get into seemingly permanent problems in the outside world, use up a disproportionate amount of staff time and energies. In small and understaffed projects, dealing with the needs of one problem child can completely unbalance carefully planned programme work.

Avoid labels

The first thing to remember is not to label the child 'disruptive' but to remember his or her individuality (which will not always be possible given the limits of human patience). Whatever decision is taken should ideally be on the basis of teamwork and discussion, in which both children and adults in the project are involved. It may be that the needs of a particularly disruptive child are due to psychiatric problems or extensive drug use that are outside the expertise and resources of your project. Perhaps he can be encouraged to find help through another project or agency.

Listen to other children

When children have a say in the day-to-day running of a project, they can often be very successful in disciplining their peers. Listen to what they have to say. Some aggressive or disruptive behaviour by unhappy children is a reaction to adults, a way of acting out their feelings about the betrayals and hypocrisy of the adult world. You may need other children to guide you through this one, although the extent to which you do so depends on the levels of participation you have reached, as discussed in the last chapter. However, listening to children's analysis of the situation can reap dividends. You may need to change the way you work.

Make a clear decision

Sometimes, after all the hard work, discussion, agonising and teamwork that have gone into trying to improve the situation for a particular boy or girl, you just have to let go. Maybe they return permanently to a life of crime, drug-taking or prostitution. Maybe you and the other children in the project decide not to let them back in. It's a hard decision, and you wonder if there was something else you could have done, something you did wrong. You still think about the days when you saw the 'good' in this child.

You have to learn that you can't win them all. You need to accept that even one good moment on one day in your project was still an improvement – even a small one – in the life of this child. The success of the project cannot always be judged by the number of children who have passed through and been 'rehabilitated', even though that is what the public, and your donors, may ask for.

You have to learn to deal with 'failure'. But you need not necessarily give up Sometimes the most disturbed children find their own way back (and maybe you *did* have something to do with it).

PROBLEMS WITH THE LAW

Projects for street and working children operate at the fringes of the law, so problems with official authorities are inevitable. As prevention is better than cure, information on legal issues gathered during the research period is vital, as are contacts with the legal profession. With this back-up you are less likely to be found running around like a headless chicken if the police come to close down your project, arrest your staff or arrest the children.

One particular issue that often arises is that income generation schemes may contravene child labour laws. In this case, you should collaborate with the 'authorities' and include a training component, so that the scheme is recognised as educational.

Drop-in centres may contravene welfare or family law because children are supposed to be living either with families or in state care. Thus you should try to get your centre accepted as a place of safety by the courts. This will also help you bail children who have been arrested out of custody into the safekeeping of the project.

If children or staff members are arrested, it is important to act quickly before they are processed by the police and courts. This may avoid their being ill-treated by the police. Quiet persistence, backed up by proper legal arguments, is the best approach. This is where prior work, learning about the law and legal system, as well as contacts made with lawyers, can reap dividends. Do you have a lawyer you can call on at night or weekends to come and work beside you to defend children or workers who are in custody? Which member of your board can be relied on to turn up at the police station and put up the money for bail?

If these approaches do not work it may be necessary to call on outside assistance, for example from an international human rights agency. But do not expect quick results from this approach. You will need to prove your own credibility and provide hard facts if the agency is to take up the case. And watch your step International agencies are not always sensitive to the fine detail of local situations, the publicity they produce and the actions they take may result in a backlash effect on your project and even worse conditions for children.

OUTREACH

Community outreach work is difficult to evaluate and can often result in simple handouts of food and advice that is sometimes dictatorial. Successful outreach means not just getting out but getting out effectively so that issues that matter to the community and the children are addressed. One of the best ways of doing this is to recruit workers directly from the community, incorporating a strong element of capacity building into the project.

With children

Outreach with individual children on a case-by-case basis, as in much street educator work, treats children out of context and increases their distance from the communities in which they live and work. The plan should not be to attract as many children as possible to a centre where they may be further stigmatised as 'street children from the project', but to work with the networks of support they already have, such as the market woman who looks after their money and the restaurant that provides them with leftover food.

With parents

Outreach with parents often begins with a contact that implicitly labels them as the failed parents of children who have run away from home or are working. Project workers must not be judgemental and should work alongside families, including other family members who are important to the child.

With communities

Outreach to the community is often limited to community leaders, who act as brokers, forming a barrier between the project and community members through which they may be able to manipulate the situation to their advantage by assuming control over the distribution of project resources. This produces a double dependency, the project is dependent on the broker for access to the community, and the community is dependent on the broker for access to resources. Although you must make contact with community leaders as a first step, recruitment of community members as workers is the second, and these need not be the people recommended by leaders, or the most educated people.

Remember that communities do not consider children to be an issue. Babies are, because of their hourly demands; youth are, because they may be regarded as a disruptive influence. But children between five and 15 years of age are invisible compared to the need for a water system, a health clinic, or women's groups (which have a voice). The key is older children and youth, who are both visible and a 'problem'. They are in contact with both children and adults and their energy can be harnessed in a leadership role.

THE PROBLEMS OF GROWTH

So many promising street children projects encounter difficulties as they grow. They begin in a small way with innovative ways of working, become organised and well known. They attract funds and international attention. The director attends meetings in other countries. Then things begin to go wrong. Management is not organised. The way the project works is no longer appropriate in changed local conditions. Funding bodies complain that reports are not good enough. Increased staff means more administration and less equality. It begins to resemble an institution. The staff complain about the director, who is always at conferences. The funding is withdrawn.

Personal involvement

It seems to be a particular characteristic of projects for street and working children that they are often personally identified with an initiator, who becomes viewed as a charismatic figure.

Unfortunately most of the information stays in the initiator's head. The requirements of good project management, not least of which is for proper accountability to donors and children, may mean that the initiator has to move on. This can be a bitter experience.

There is no growth without pain, and yet this problem can be avoided by following the steps outlined in this manual, basing a project on well-founded research, record-keeping, participatory planning, management and evaluation.

It may be that the best person to attend a conference is not the director or initiator, but the worker on the team with the best experience in the topic of the conference. And don't let language problems stop the real expert attending because he or she cannot speak English; if you insist, most conference organisers can find a means of translating. The experience of travel abroad, and meeting people from other projects and other countries, is a valuable part of staff development.

The expansion of Street Wise has meant that staff are often under considerable pressure. The boys must be cared for or kept occupied for twenty four hours a day. The costs of running such programmes are huge, and considerable effort must be invested in fund raising (Summing Up, p19).

Too little growth

As they become better known, small projects suffer from demands to provide more services or to serve more children.

If the resources are not available, remember that you cannot be all things to all people:

- Stick to what you are good at.
- Plan for expansion realistically.
- Collaborate and share with other NGOs.
- Advocate for better treatment for children.
- Recognise the problems that are outside your scope (as in the case of YUVA and the drug abusers).

Too much growth

As they become better known, small projects may be seen as successful and swamped with money (and publicity) before they are really experienced.

- Don't be reliant on external donors, who may put their own demands on your programme.
- Don't allow the initiator to go globe-trotting.
- Don't present yourselves as experts in the whole field of street or working children worldwide; the beginning of wisdom is knowing how ignorant you are.

Fundraising

Too often the planning process begins with thinking about external resources, which:

- creates dependency that may be short-lived, as most international donors fund for three years only;
- parallels begging;
- can lead to projects being led by funding considerations rather than children's needs ('SCF is keen on income generation at the moment, so that is what we must have, or that is what we must call it').

A truly local, sustainable project starts from the local problem, the local solution and the local resources. External finance should be used only to start up the project, so that novel ways of working can either be shown to work and attract funds from local resources, or generate sufficient income for the project to be self-supporting. This means drawing up budgets that show a decreasing input from external funders over time:

- Aim for local self-sufficiency not dependency.
- Raise money locally.
- Use local resources.
- Plan for growth within your budget.
- Dont stagger on from one three-year grant to another.
- Dont be 'finance led' by external donors.

An important aspect of fundraising may well consist of educating donors, both local and international about the lives of children you work with and the best ways of meeting their needs. This is where both initial research and ongoing monitoring operate to support project development.

PROGRAMME ISSUES

Transfer to formal school

Children transferring from a non-formal education project to school may need help with fees, uniforms and books. Schemes for loans and grants can be developed, often with funds raised by the local community on an annual basis.

Some children may not have a birth certificate which is required for school registration. This is serious as the effects are lifelong. Without a birth certificate people have no official identity and may be excluded from all but casual labour as well as from being able to vote.

Children are entitled to an identity by the provision of Articles 7 and 8 of the Convention on the Rights of the Child.

It may be that children without birth certificates were never registered, or that the details of registration have been forgotten, or they may have lost contact with the parents who registered them.

An interim solution that enables these children to enter school may be possible. In Sri Lanka SCF programme staff take children without certificates to doctors who estimate their ages and provide the documentation through which the Registrar General's office will provide a 'Certificate of Probable Age' with which children can enter school. However, efforts to locate lost birth registration should not end, because this document is vital for future life chances, almost always controlling access to formal employment.

If there are no mechanisms by which children without birth certificates can be given an identity, this is an opportunity for advocacy work.

Moving on

One thing is certain, street and working children eventually grow into young people. There is almost no research about what happens to street children when they grow up, and few projects have thought through the question of what will happen to children who grow too old for the project.

'Now the time has come to cater for street youth,' is what Joseph Junior, director of the Bombay forum for street children, can be heard to say these days. Similarly, at The Concerned for Working Children in Bangalore the programme was forced to change by young people who expressed their feelings of hurt at being obliged to leave the project that had sheltered them, because of their age. They had nowhere else to go, and they felt rejected.

Boys from YUVA in Bombay found their own solution, a group renting a joint place to live. Projects can encourage this with housing loans, help with life skills (do they know how to wash their own clothes, shop and cook, save and pay bills, deal with the day-to-day problems of house maintenance?), advice and support. Temporary 'move-on' accommodation can be provided while young people find their feet, and this could be linked with a youth housing scheme if there is one.

Whatever the scheme, make sure that children know what the next step will be, and help them make the decision about this by discussing choices. If they all go from your project to another project they are continuing to be institutionalised, which is neat but not developmental.

It is good for children who have left the project as 'successes', moving on to school, work and family life, to return for visits. They have a point of personal reference as they grow, and it is excellent for staff morale. But you also need to 'let go', accepting that the project was only a stage in their lives and a step to better things. Above all, resist the impulse to exhibit successes for publicity or fundraising.

Dealing with injury and death

The lives of disadvantaged children are often dangerous. It is inevitable that some of the children you work with will be hurt, or even die. This is painful for both children and project workers.

When children are injured, or particularly if they die, the project needs to confront the feelings of anger and guilt that are a normal part of grieving, for both workers and children.

Death should be dealt with by:
- helping children to mark their loss publicly by, for instance, attending the funeral, or visiting the grave;

- staff talking about their feelings through the usual support mechanisms of the project;
- staff encouraging children to talk about their feelings;
- trying to ensure that, if the child's death was preventable, the facts are placed before the proper authorities. It may be that children can learn about advocacy through such a process, as in the case of the Bhima Sangha investigation into child deaths in Sivakasi firework factories;
- if the child died of a preventable illness, making sure that children know about this illness and how to protect themselves.

Injury, illness and death actually provide opportunities for children to learn:
- about how safety can be improved;
- about how to protect themselves;
- about how to take control of their own lives, not being victims.

Dealing with theft from and damage to the project

One of the most demoralising and frequent crises faced by projects for street children arises when children steal or damage property that was provided for their welfare. It hurts.

First you need to assess the damage:
- to actual property;
- to staff self-esteem;
- to other children;
- to the project's resources;
- to the relationships between the culprits and the project.

Then you need to think about why the damage occurred. Was it really the children, or:
- was it outsiders, or children excluded from the project, trying to break in?
- was it outside older youth who resent the project removing the power they had previously enjoyed over younger children who are now in the project?
- was it the police or the public trying to destroy the project because they are afraid of the children or do not understand what the project is trying to do?

Each of these possibilities suggests an answer in terms of public relations and outreach work, and also the need to talk the incident over with children.

If the thief is from the project, or damage was caused by children in the project, why did this happen?
- Did they steal out of greed or need?
- Did they steal out of envy?

- Did they steal because the project or the workers seem to be rich, so they won't miss things, or they can always buy more?
- Was the damage the result of play that got out of hand?
- Were the culprits under the influence of drink or drugs?
- Was it an act of anger? If so, what was the cause of the anger?
- Were they destroying something important to them because it seemed too good to be true?

You will only find out about the motivation behind theft and damage in a particular case if you listen to children. Your reaction is important, as are the steps you are seen to take to ensure that justice is done and the damage is repaired, not just in terms of property but also the people involved and community atmosphere in the project.

Children need to be involved in the internal process of justice, as part of their developing participation in the project. They can be involved at all stages of this process:

- assessing damage;
- finding out who is to blame;
- helping to understand why they did it;
- deciding on what action to take with the culprits;
- repairing the damage.

If the damage is substantial, this may involve insurance claims and have to be reported to the police, insurers and funding bodies. This is where you really need a supportive board of management.

Finally, remember that such damage happens in all projects and can mean many things. It may be that you are on the right track, or that you need to change what you are doing, that one child you have been working with has particular problems or that you were in the wrong place at the wrong time. Within a reasonable period of time the project team should evaluate the incident and the way it was dealt with, as well as any adjustments to the project that were made as a consequence.

Then pick yourself up, dust yourself off and start all over again.

A FINAL WORD

When bad things happen it is all too easy to feel the work is not worthwhile, and to want to give up Some workers will leave. It may be time for them to move on. The work is exhausting and can disrupt all the other relationships in your life.

But it is almost always the case that, just when a low point is reached, something happens to remind you of success as well as failure. These insights tend to come from the children – a small gift, a gesture from one boy to show that he notices you are depressed and he cares, a smiling wave from across the street from a girl who left the project last year and is doing well in school, a boy who comes back after a long absence to bring back the money he owes you.

You will somehow always find that it *is* worth carrying on.

REFERENCES

Aptekar, L, *Street children of Cali*, Durham & London, Duke University Press, 1988.

Barker, G & Mbogori, E, *Aids awareness and prevention with Kenyan street youth: results of a qualitative research project*, Childhope USA working paper No. 4, in collaboration with the Undugu Society, 1992.

Bequele, A, 'Combating child labour: contrasting views and strategies for very poor countries', in ILO, *Conditions of Work Digest*, Vol 10, No.1, Geneva, International Labour Office, 1991.

Bequele, A & Boyden, J, 'Child labour: problems, policies and programmes', in Bequele, A & Boyden, J (eds), *Combating child labour*, Geneva, International Labour Office, 1988.

Black, M, *Innocenti Global Seminar: street and working children*, 15-25 February 1993, Florence, Italy. Summary report, Florence, Unicef, 1993.

Bonnerjea, L, *Family tracing: a good practice guide*, London, Save the Children Development Manual, No. 3, 1994.

Boyden, J, 'National policies and programmes for childworkers: Peru', in Bequele, A & Boyden, J (eds), *Combating child labour*, Geneva, International Labour Office, 1988.

Boyden, J, 'Childhood and the policy makers: a comparative perspective on the globalization of childhood', in James, A & Prout, A (eds), *Constructing and deconstructing childhood: contemporary issues in the sociological study of childhood*, London, New York, Philadelphia, The Falmer Press, 1990.

Burra, N, 'A report on child labour in the lock industry of Aligarh, Uttar Pradesh, India', prepared for Unicef, New Delhi, unpublished, 1987.

Connolly, M, 'Surviving the streets', in *AIDS Action*, Issue 11, London, AHRTAG, 1990a.

Connolly, M, 'Adrift in the city: a comparative study of street children in Bogotá, Colombia, and Guatemala City', in Boxill, N A (ed), *Homeless children: the watchers and the waiters*, New York, The Haworth Press, 1990b.

Connolly, M, *The health of street children and youth*, Survivors Series No.1, New York, Unicef, 1994.

Dallape, F, *An experience with street children*, Nairobi, Undugu Society, 1988.

Dallape, F & Gilbert, C, *Children's participation in action research: a training course for trainers*, Harare, Zimbabwe, ENDA, 1993.

D'Lima, H & Gosalia, R, *Street children in Bombay: a situational analysis*, New Delhi, National Labour Office, 1992.

Ennew, J, 'Young hustlers: work and childhood in Jamaica', Report for the Overseas Development Administration, unpublished, 1982.

Ennew, J & Milne, B, *The next generation: lives of third world children*, London, Zed Books Ltd, 1989.

Ennew, J & Young, P, *Child labour in Jamaica*, London, Anti-Slavery Society, 1982.

George, M, 'Children in employment in Peninsular Malaysia', in Jomo, K S (ed), *Child labour in Malaysia*, Kuala Lumpur, Forum, Selanga Malaysia for Labour Studies Programme, Institute of Advanced Studies, University of Malaysia, 1992.

Glauser, B, 'Street children: deconstructing a construct', in James, A & Prout, A (eds), *Constructing and deconstructing childhood: contemporary issues in the sociological study of childhood*, London, New York, Philadelphia, The Falmer Press, 1990.

Gosling, L & Edwards, M, *Assessment, monitoring, review and evaluation: toolkits*, London, Save the Children Development Manual Series, 1994.

Gunn, S & Ostos, Z, 'Dilemmas in tackling child labour: the case of scavenger children in the Philippines', in *International Labour Review*, Vol 131, No.6, 629-646, 1992.

Hart, R, *Children's participation: from tokenism to citizenship*, Innocenti Essays No.4, Florence, Unicef, 1992.

Kumar, K, *The child's language and the teacher: a handbook*, New Delhi, Unicef, 1987.

Lusk, M, 'Street children programs in Latin America', *Journal of Sociology and Social Welfare*, Vol 16, No.1, 55-77, 1989.

Molaké: *Molaké* (Sprout) is the quarterly journal of The Concerned for Working Children, Bangalore, India.

Myers, W (ed), *Protecting working children*, London, New Jersey, Zed Books Ltd, 1991.

Nieuwenhuys, O, *Children's lifeworlds: gender, welfare and labour in the developing world*, London, New York, Routledge, 1994.

Oloko, B A, 'Children's domestic versus economic work and school achievement', unpublished paper, 1990.

Oxfam, *The Field Directors' Handbook: an Oxfam manual for development workers*, edited by Brian Pratt and Jo Boyden, Oxford, Oxford University Press, 1985.

Pangan, A M L, 'A study of coping patterns of children living in dump sites of Metro Manila, Philippines', unpublished paper for Conference on Children at Risk, University of Bergen, 13-14 May 1992.

Phillips, W S K, *Street children of Indore: a situational analysis*, New Delhi, National Labour Institute, 1992.

Proceedings: *Proceedings of the First Metro Manila Street Children's Conference*, Manila, National Council of Social Development, 29-31 May 1990.

Reddy, N, *Street children of Bangalore: a situational analysis*, New Delhi, National Labour Institute, 1992.

Reynolds, P, *Dance Civet Cat: child labour in the Zambezi valley*, Zimbabwe, Baobab Books; London, Zed Books Ltd; Athens, Ohio, Ohio University Press,1990.

Rogers, G & Standing, G, *Childwork, poverty and underdevelopment*, Geneva, ILO, 1981.

Street children in Asia: *Mobilizing community action for street children*, First regional conference/seminar on street children in Asia, Manila, Childhope International, 4-13 May 1989.

Summing Up: *Summing up of our experiences in work with street children*, Roisin Burke, Dale Chandler, Stanley Dhlamini, Kirk Felsman, Andreas Fuglesang, Celine Gilbert, Grethe Gulliksen, Godfrey Kawome, Mike Lynch, Richard Macharia Komu, Josephat Mathe, Monica Monro, Maxwell Rupondo, Abubakar Sultan, Lellem Tukuye, Nadia Ahmed Mohammed Zaid, Teddy Zulu, Zimbabwe, Redd Barna Africa, 1990.

Swart, J, 'An anthropological study of street children in Hillbrow, Johannesburg, with special reference to their moral values', MA thesis in anthropology, University of South Africa, unpublished, 1988.

Swart, J, *Malunde: the street children of Hillbrow*, Johannesburg, Witwatersrand University Press, 1990.

Taçon, P, 'A Unicef response to the needs of abandoned and street children', unpublished, Geneva, Unicef, 1985.

Tolfree, D, *Roofs and roots: the care of separated children in the third world*, London, Arena Press, 1995 forthcoming.

Tyler et al: Tyler, F B, Tyler, S L, Tomasello, A & Connolly, M R, 'Huckleberry Finn and street youth everywhere: an approach to primary prevention', in Albee, G W, Bond, L A & Cook Munsey, T V, *Global perspectives on prevention: primary prevention of psychopathology*, Vol XLV, Sage Publications, 200-212, 1992.

Unicef, *State of the world's children, 1988*, Oxford, Oxford University Press, 1987.

WCEFA, World Conference on Education for All, background document, *Meeting basic learning needs: a vision for the 1990s*, New York, Unicef, 1990.

Weisner, T S, 'Cultural and universal aspects of social support for children', in Belle, D (ed), *Children, social networks and social support*, New York, John Wiley, 1989.

What's Inside?: *What's Inside? learning with children on the streets*, Gunesekera, M, Fernando, R, Indralatha, W D C & Perera, A L L P, edited by Fuglesang, A & Chandler, D, Sri Lanka, Redd Barna, 1989.

Working in the streets: *Working in the streets: working children in Asunción*, Espinola, B, Glauser, B, Ortiz, R M & Ortiz de Carrizosa, S, Methological Series No. 4, Bogotá, Unicef.

Wright, J D, Kaminsky, D & Wittig, M, 'Health and social conditions of street children in Honduras', *American Journal of the Diseases of Children*, Vol 147, 279-283, 1993.

APPENDIX 1: Checklist and flow chart for planning

Do you know what you and your staff think is:
- an ideal childhood
- a street child
- harmful work for children
- children's rights
- child participation?

Do you know what the local ideas are about:
- an ideal childhood
- a street child
- the work that children should do
- children's rights?

Has the country in which you are going to work:
- signed and ratified ILO Convention 138 and Recommendation 46
- signed and ratified the Convention on the Rights of the Child?

Is there a country report to the Committee on the Rights of the Child?
Is there an alternative report?
What do these say about street children and child work?
What is the national legislation relevant to street and working children?
Do you have information about children in general, and street and working children from:
- national government
- local government
- academics
- Unicef, WHO and ILO
- other NGOs?

What more do you need to know?
What methods will you use to research the local situation?
Are you starting with observation and moving on to other methods?
Will you work with an outside researcher? Have you agreed terms and methods with him/her?
How will children participate in the research?

Have you analysed all the information you have and identified:
- a target group
- a gap in provision
- ways of cooperating with other NGOs?

What are the objectives of your project?
What indicators will you use to check if the objectives are achieved?
Will your project include:
- service provision
- development
- advocacy?

What methods will you use to work with children, parents and communities? (refer to the checklist at the end of chapter 5, p127)
How will the work be recorded and evaluated?
What type of staff will you need?
Do you have a plan for the first three years of operation?
Do you have a budget for this?
How will you raise the initial funds?
Does your plan include moving towards local self-sufficiency?
What kind of management structure will work best?
What links with outside bodies will provide extra expertise for specific parts of the project?
What links with official bodies do you have – for example, with:
- local government
- schools
- hospitals and clinics
- police?

Have you made links with lawyers who will be able to support you in your work?
Does your board of management understand what you are trying to do?
If they do not, what steps are you taking to educate them?
What links do members of the board have with official bodies and commerce?
Does the board include representatives of staff, communities and children?
Have you a plan for the progressive participation of children in:
- planning the project
- the operation of the project
- evaluatiing the project?

Have you a plan for staff development?
Does this include volunteers, the cook, driver, watchman etc?

Have you plans for:
- staff support
- discipline (staff and children)
- standards of work, dress and behaviour?

Are these agreed with the staff?
Are they flexible?
What steps have you taken for regular review of methods, plans and structure?

FLOW CHART FOR PLANNING

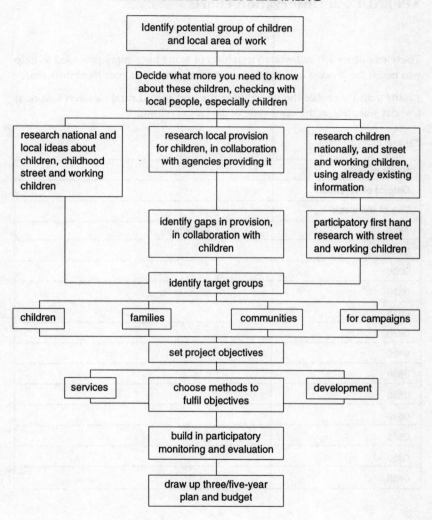

Identify potential group of children
and local area of work

Decide what more you need to know
about these children, checking with
local people, especially children

research national and
local ideas about
children, childhood
street and working
children

research local provision
for children, in collaboration
with agencies providing it

research children
nationally, and street
and working children,
using already existing
information

identify gaps in provision,
in collaboration with
children

participatory first hand
research with street
and working children

identify target groups

children   families   communities   for campaigns

set project objectives

services   choose methods to
fulfil objectives   development

build in participatory
monitoring and evaluation

draw up three/five-year
plan and budget

APPENDIX 2: Observation charts

These examples are *not* written in tablets of stone but simply provided to help you begin the process of designing your own charts to fit your local situation.

Charts 1 and *2* enable the user to monitor and record rural children's work at five-day intervals, at the same time of day, for one hour.

Chart 1

Name of child	
Date of observation	
Day of the week	
Time	Activity
0800	
0805	
0810	
0815	
0820	
0825	
0830	
0835	
0840	
0845	
0850	
0855	

Chart 2

Name of child			
Date of observation			
Day of the week			
Time	Childcare	Cooking	Playing

Chart 3

This chart enables the user to record the activities of a group of street children around a bus station. (The chart can be adapted by the user to monitor activity in other similar environments.)

Date									
Location									
Time					From:		To:		
Child	Talking	Mixing with adults	Playing	Gambling	Selling	Stealing	Drugs	Other
Juan								
Marco								
Jesus								
Raul								
Henri								
Other(s)								

APPENDIX 3: Further reading and resources

(1) Accounts of experiences with street and working children

The following is a list of the most accessible and readable works dealing either with research or project experiences. The notes provide a brief indication of the content and uses, and how to obtain the book or article. Addresses of the organisations mentioned will be found in Appendix 4. Where possible the international reference number for books (ISBN) has been included, to help when ordering from bookshops and libraries.

Aptekar, L, *Street children of Cali*, Durham & London, Duke University Press, 1988.
  A comprehensive book about the author's research in Colombia, using psychological and anthropological methods and challenging many of the myths. Includes a bibliography. Can be obtained on order from bookshops and libraries, ISBN 0-8223-0834-7.

Bequele, A & Boyden, J, Child labour: problems, policies and programmes, in Bequele, A & Boyden, J (eds), *Combating child labour*, Geneva, International Labour Office, 1988.
  A book of readings from the early 1980s, the paper by William Myers on alternative programmes for street children (pp125-144) is a classic resource for programme planning. Jo Boyden's paper on policies and programmes in Peru (pp195-216) shows the usefulness of researching the NGO sector. Other papers are of very variable quality. Order photocopies of the articles from an academic library or order the book from the ILO. ISBN 92-2-106389-5 (hardback) or 92-2-106388-7 (paperback).

Dallape, F, *An experience with street children*, Nairobi, Undugu Society, 1988.
  This book, which has been used extensively as source material for this manual, is available from the Undugu Society, a well-established street and working children programme in Kenya.

Ennew, J (ed), *Learning or labouring? essential readings in child labour as it relates to basic education*, Florence, Unicef, 1994.
  A book of readings from key works on child work, child labour and education, intended as a resource book for project managers. Order from Unicef, Florence.

Gunn, S & Ostos, Z, Dilemmas in tackling child labour: the case of scavenger children in the Philippines, in *International Labour Review*, Vol 131, No.6, 629-646, 1992.
This account of the development of the SABANA project has been referred to several times in the manual. A photocopy of the article can be ordered from any academic library. Or write to the International Labour Office (ILO).

Nieuwenhuys, O, *Children's lifeworlds: gender, welfare and labour in the developing world*, London & New York, Routledge, 1994.
An academic but readable account of research in Kerala, India, with rural child workers. Includes a good discussion of the difference between work and labour, and an extensive bibliography. Can be ordered from bookshops and libraries. ISBN 0-415-09750-9 (hardback) 0-415-09751 (paperback).

Reynolds, P, *Dance Civet Cat: child labour in the Zambezi Valley*, Zimbabwe, Baobab Books; London, Zed Books Ltd; Athens, Ohio, Ohio University Press, 1990.
A description of academic research on child labour in rural Zimbabwe. Particularly useful for the explanation of methods used and their relative usefulness. Includes an extensive bibliography. Can be ordered from bookshops and libraries. ISBN 0-86232-932-9 (hardback) 0-86232-933-7 (paperback).

Summing Up: *Summing up of our experiences in work with street children*, Roisin Burke, Dale Chandler, Stanley Dhlamini, Kirk Felsman, Andreas Fuglesang, Celine Gilbert, Grethe Gulliksen, Godfrey Kawome, Mike Lynch, Richard Macharia Komu, Josephat Mathe, Monica Monro, Maxwell Rupondo, Abubakar Sultan, Lellem Tukuye, Nadia Ahmed Mohammed Zaid, Teddy Zulu, Zimbabwe, Redd Barna Africa, 1990.
This is a brief account of a workshop in which a number of projects in Africa shared their experiences (both good and bad). Can be obtained from Redd Barna in Norway.

Swart, J, *Malunde: the street children of Hillbrow*, Johannesburg, Witwatersrand University Press, 1990.
A very readable account of research carried out by the initiator of the Street Wise project, containing information about children's lives, the methods used and a bibliography. Can be ordered from bookshops and libraries. ISBN 1-86814-1225.

What's Inside?: *What's Inside? learning with children on the streets*, Gunesekera, M, Fernando, R, Indralatha, W D C & Perera, A L L P, edited by Fuglesang A & Chandler, D, Sri Lanka, Redd Barna, 1989.
A very honest account of the early work of this interesting project, including descriptions of innovative methods. Best to ignore the information in the appendices, which is not all accurate. Can be obtainedfrom Redd Barna in Norway.

Working in the streets: *Working in the streets: working children in Asuncion*, Espinola, B, Glauser, B, Ortiz, R M & Ortiz de Carrizosa, S, Methodological Series No. 4, Bogotá, Unicef.
A lively account of research carried out by the project Callescuela in the early

1980s. As an account of the lives of working street children this has no equal. Also available in the original Spanish as *En la calle* (the English translation is not as good). Should be obtainable from Unicef Regional Office in Bogotá.

Wright, J D, Kaminsky, D & Wittig, M, Health and social conditions of street children in Honduras, *American Journal of the Diseases of Children*, Vol 147, 279-283, 1993.
An academic account of the children served by Project Alternatives in Honduras. Should be possible to order as a photocopy from an academic library.

YUVA, *Life on the mean streets: experiences of working with street children*, Bombay, Youth for Unity and Voluntary Action, 1992.
A brief, but illuminating and honest account of the early work of the organisation YUVA in Bombay. Available from YUVA.

There are five journals of particular interest for those working with street and working children. These are:

A Letter from the Street, is the newsletter of ENDA a networking organisation that is particularly active in Africa, and published in French and English.

Child Workers in Asia, gives a round-up of news and information in Asian countries, available on subscription from Child Workers in Asia.

International Children's Rights Monitor, the quarterly journal of Defence for Children International (DCI), which frequently gives information about street and working children and also provides news of conferences and new publications worldwide.

Molaké (Sprout) is the quarterly journal of The Concerned for Working Children, Bangalore, India, but has a global perspective.

NATS, which deals exclusively with street and working children, and is published in Spanish and English. Details from MLAL.

(2) Planning issues

The following list contains either key texts or works of reference that contain bibliographies or resource lists from which you can widen your reading and resources.

(i) Research

Dallape, F & Gilbert, C, *Children's participation in action research: a training course for trainers*, Harare, Zimbabwe, ENDA, 1993.
Guidelines derived from a course run by ENDA, resulting in a practical, easy-to-follow introduction to carrying out research *with* rather than on street and working children. Providing many useful examples as well as an explanation of

the participatory approach, this guide, like the two accompanying volumes (see below) is essential reading. Available from ENDA, copies are free but postage must be paid, the cost of air mail to Europe for one copy is about US$4 (see also Gosling & Edwards, below).

Pratt, B & Loizos, P, *Choosing research methods: data collection for development workers*, Development Guidelines No. 7, Oxford, Oxfam, 1992.
A very practical and accessible guide to research methods, available from Oxfam, 274, Banbury Road, Oxford OX2 7DZ, United Kingdom.

(ii) Planning and evaluation

Dallape, F & Gilbert, C, *Alternative education, savings and credit and project management*, Harare, Zimbabwe, ENDA, 1994.
Another excellent practical guide that can be read and appreciated at any level of education, for ordering details see Dallape & Gilbert above.

Gosling, L & Edwards, M, *Assessment, monitoring, review and evaluation: toolkits*, London, Save the Children Development Manual Series, 1994.
A detailed review of the entire participatory planning process, from initial thoughts to evaluation, that can be used as a guide for project managers at all levels.

Myers, W E (ed), *Protecting working children*, London, Zed Books Ltd, 1991.
A book of readings that contains some research results and planning experiences. Most useful are the articles on planning approaches by William Myers, and the influential article on participatory evaluation of street children projects in Brazil by Thereza Penna Firme and her collaborators. Available from Zed Books Ltd, 7 Cynthia Street, London N1 9JF. The cost of the paperback is $19.95 plus $3.50 for postage and packing.

(iii) Specific programme issues
There are few books giving practical guidance on projects for street and working children. The following is a mixed bag of practical writings that can lead either to further reading or to more ideas.

AHRTAG and the Brazilian Center for the Defense of Rights of Children and Adolescents, *Resource pack on sexual health and Aids prevention for socially apart youth*, London, AHRTAG, 1993.
AHRTAG (Appropriate Health Resources & Technologies Action Group) is an international development NGO that promotes primary health care. It has a resource centre of primary health care materials, runs an information service and produces newsletters, manuals and other publications. This is a comprehensive and easy to use resource pack, available free to groups concerned with socially apart youth in developing countries and for $10 (including postage) to others. Obtainable from AHRTAG.

Beers, H van, *In search of the girl: a critical review of the literature on girlhood in the south*, Amsterdam, InDRA Occasional Paper No. 2, 1994.
> A well-researched guide to the available literature, published and unpublished, on this topic, with sections on work, street girls and sexual exploitation. Available from InDRA, University of Amsterdam, Plantage Muidergracht 12, 1018 TV Amsterdam, The Netherlands.

Bonnerjea, L, *Family tracing: a good practice guide*, London, Save the Children Development Manual No. 3, 1994.
> Available from Save the Children, London.

Child-to Child, *Activity Sheets*, and *Resource Book*.
> Child-to-Child is an approach to health education and primary health care working through a network of health and education workers in over 60 countries. It involves children in health education and has materials, for children and health workers, translated into various languages, including Arabic, Chinese, French, Gujarati, Hindi, Indonesian, Portuguese, Sesotho, Spanish, Swahili and Telegu. One of the activity sheets concerns street children directly and others are relevant. The resource book contains a section 'ideas into action' that is useful for training in participatory methods of work.

Connolly, M, *The health of street children and youth*, Survivors Series No.1, New York, Unicef, 1994.
> A factual survey of health problems for street children worldwide, including consideration of the effectiveness of different programme approaches.

Dallape, F & Gilbert, C, *Children and the urban crisis, options for the future: a training course for trainers*, Harare, Zimbabwe, ENDA.
> Deals with the training of street educators, a companion volume to the two already listed by the same authors and available from the same source.

Ennew, J (ed), *Street and working children: a resource file*.
> A selection of readings and a resource list, for use by project workers at all levels. Available from Save the Children, London.

Freire, P, *Pedagogy of the oppressed*, and *Literacy in 36 hours*.
> Both classic, inspirational texts from the Brazilian educator, whose work has been influential in adult literacy work worldwide, and in the development of the 'street educator' philosophy in Latin America. A volume published by Unicef's Bogotá office (*Paulo Freire and the street educators*) records a confrontation between Freire and some of the proponents of street education. *Pedagogy of the oppressed*, has been translated into several languages and reprinted many times. It is slightly academic and very rhetorical, but worth reading, *Literacy in 36 hours* is also available in many editions, and more readable. Neither deals directly with children.

Kumar, K, *The child's language and the teacher: a handbook*, New Delhi, Unicef, 1987.
Although written on the basis of activities carried out in Madhya Pradesh, India, this book has universal significance as a guide to non-formal education methods and philosophy for teachers. It is readable and eminently practical, with many examples but also written in such a way that readers are likely to come up with many other classroom ideas of their own. Still available on request from Unicef, New York or New Delhi.

Werner, D with Thurman, C & Maxwell J, *Where there is no doctor: a village health care handbook*, California, The Hesperian Foundation, 1992.
The classic text on primary health care, accessible to readers and users at all levels. No project should be without it. Translated into Spanish also. Available from TALC (Teaching Aids at Low Cost), which has a good list of other useful titles available.

World Health Organisation (WHO), *One way street?*, Geneva, WHO Programme on Substance Abuse, 1993.
The first report of the project on street children and substance abuse. Also available in French and Spanish. Contains interesting details of various programmes and some factual data, also a description of the use of focus group discussion methods of research.

APPENDIX 4: Useful addresses

AHRTAG
Farringdon Point
29-35 Farringdon Road
London EC1M 3JB
United Kingdom
Tel: 071-242 0606
Fax: 071-242 0041

ANPPCAN (African Network for the Prevention and Protection against Child Abuse
and Neglect)
PO Box 71240
Nairobi
Kenya

Anti-Slavery International
Unit 4
The Stableyard
Broomgrove Road
London SW9
United Kingdom

Child Rights ASIANET
Faculty of Law
Chulalongkorn University
Phyathai Road
Bangkok
Thailand

Child-to-Child Trust
Room 632
Institute of Education
20 Bedford Way
London WC1H 0AL
United Kingdom

Childwatch International
PO Box 1096
Blindern
N-0317 Oslo
Norway

Child Workers in Asia
4/68 Mooban Tawanna
Soi Puak Road
Vipawadi Rangsit Road
Bangkok 10900
Thailand

[The] Concerned for Working Children
303/2 L.B. ShastrinagarDoopanahalli
Vimanapura Port
Annasandrapalya
Bangalore – 560017
India
Tel: 527258

Defence for Children International (International Section)
3 rue de Varembe
CH-1211 Geneva
Switzerland

ENDA Jeunesse Action
PO Box 3370
Dakar
Senegal

ENDA Training Programme
PO Box A 113
Harare
Zimbabwe

ENDA – Zimbabwe
PO Box 3492
Harare
Zimbabwe

International Labour Office (ILO)
International Programme for the Elimination of Child Labour (IPEC)
Section for child work and vulnerable workers
4 route des Morillons
CH-1211 Geneva 22
Switzerland

MANTHOC
Corazeros 260
Pueblo Libre
Lima
Peru

MLAL
vicolo s Domenico 11
37 100 Verona
Italy

Oxfam
274 Banbury Road
Oxford OX2 7DZ
United Kingdom

Redd Barna (Norwegian Save the Children)
Grensesvingen 7
PO Box 6200 Etterstad
N - 0602 Oslo 6
Norway

Save the Children (UK)
Mary Datchelor House
17 Grove Lane
Camberwell
London SE5 8RD
United Kindom

TALC (Teaching Aids at Low Cost)
PO Box 49
St Albans
Herts AL1 4AX
United Kingdom

Unesco
Education Programme for Street and Working Children
Unit for Inter-agency Cooperation in Basic Education
Education Sector
7 Place de Fontenoy
75352 Paris
France

Unicef
The following are the main points of reference for obtaining further information from
Unicef:

(1) Headquarters
Publications Division
Unicef
Three United Nations Plaza
New York, NY 10017
USA

(2) International Child Development Centre
Piazza SS Annunziata 12
50122 Florence
Italy

United Nations Human Rights Commission
Palais des Nations
CH-1211 Geneva
Switzerland

World Health Organisation
Programme on Substance Abuse
Global Programme on AIDS
20 Avenue Appia
CH-1211 Geneva 27
Switzerland

YUVA (Youth for Unity and Voluntary Action)
8 Ground Floor
33L Mugbat Cross Lane
Bombay – 400 004
India

NOTES

NOTES

NOTES

NOTES

NOTES

NOTES

NOTES

Other Save the Children development manuals

Save the Children development manuals are short practical guides for field staff overseas in particular areas of fieldwork. The manuals draw on field experiences within a particular country, countries or regions.
ISSN: 0966-6982

Family tracing
A good practice guide
Lucy Bonnerjea
Development manual 3
£4.95   1994   A5 paperback   124 pages   ISBN 1 870322 77 0

Communicating with children
Helping children in distress
Naomi Richman
Development manual 2
£3.95   1993   A5 paperback   108 pages   ISBN 1 870322 49 5

Helping children in difficult circumstances
A teacher's manual
Naomi Richman
Development manual 1
£2.95   1991   A5 paperback   48 pages   ISBN 1 870322 42 8